A
Setback
IS A
Setup
FOR A
Comeback!

Now Is the Time to Make a Comeback!

Willie Jolley

GOKO
MANAGEMENT

This book is dedicated to my mother,
Catherine B. Jolley, for her years of
personal sacrifice so my brother and I
could get a quality education, and for
her constant encouragement in every
project I have ever undertaken.
God truly is a good God for blessing
us with a mother like you!
And also to my father, Levi H. Jolley,
who died so early, yet taught us so much!

GOKO Management
ACN 002 530 298

Level 8, 182–186 Blues Point Road
McMahons Point NSW 2060, Australia
Phone: (612) 9922 5334
Facsimile: (612) 9922 5343
Email: info@goko.com.au
Australian & New Zealand Distributors

Quote from Benjamin Mays on p. xiii is
being reprinted with permission from
Quotable Quotes © 1983 by Dr. Benjamin Mays.

Library of Congress Cataloguing-in-Publication Data

Jolley, Willie.
    A setback is a setup for a comeback : turn your moments of doubt and fear
into times of triumph / Willie Jolley.—2nd ed.
    p. cm.
    ISBN 0-957-8081-5-1
    1. Success—Psychological aspects. 2. Problem solving.
I. Title.
BF637.S8J63   1999
158.1—dc21   99-15903
                                                    CIP

First Edition: October 1999
Second Edition: January 2002

10 9 8 7 6 5 4 3 2

Turn your moments of doubt and fear into times of triumph

A setback is nothing but a setup for a comeback! The wisdom in these words can help lift you out of your low points in life and put you on the path to victory!

- Have you ever had a setback?

- Has life ever thrown you a curve ball?

- Have you ever been knocked down by hard times?

Willie Jolley the author of the motivational bestseller *It Only Takes a Minute to Change Your Life!*, will inspire you to take action! In *A Setback Is a Setup for a Comeback*, Willie presents his "VDAD" formula (Vision, Decision, Action, Desire) for overcoming life's constant challenges. He shares his techniques for taking control of your destiny, using anecdotes and stories that will encourage you to focus and take action on your dreams—despite the adversities! You will hear from ordinary people who refused to cower in the face of hardships and found opportunities in unlikely places. There are humourous insights ("Sometimes you're the windshield, sometimes you're the bug") and practical methods ("Need to rid yourself of negative thoughts? Face it, trace it, erase it, replace it!"). Using Willie Jolley's twelve simple strategies (as outlined in the VDAD formula) will enable you to turn your trials into triumphs, your problems into possibilities, and your setbacks into comebacks!

Also by Willie Jolley

It Only Takes a Minute to Change Your Life!

Acknowledgments

◇ ◇ ◇ First, I want to thank my friend and my father, my mentor and my master, my help and my hope, my light and my Lord, my guide and my God . . . His name is Jesus, and I am so thankful for all that He has done for me! I thank my wife Dee, who is not just my wife and love of my life, but also my best friend, and doubles as a great copy editor and business partner. I want to thank my children, William and Sherry Latoya, for their love and support, in all my endeavors. Thanks to my brother Noble and his family for their great faith and support. And thanks to my in-laws, Rivers Sr., Rivers Jr., Edith and Shirley Taylor for their encouragement and support.

I am very thankful for all the people who contributed to this book. I want to thank everyone I interviewed; everyone who submitted stories; and all the people whose stories have inspired me through the years. I convey a special thanks to all my readers, Rhonda Davis Smith, David Metcalf, RaeCarol Flynn, Darlene Bryant, and Brad and Terry Thomas. And a thank you to the Chevy Chase Regional Library in Washington, D.C., for letting me "camp out" and work on this book in peace and quiet.

Thank you, thank you, thank you to everyone at St. Martin's Press. The publishers, the sales team, the publicity people, and everyone in the office, you are all wonderful—especially the person I consider the best editor in the world, Jennifer Enderlin.

I must give a big thank you to my friend and super agent, Jeff Herman, for getting me to St. Martin's and for making sure that people around the globe were able to read the words and ideas of Willie Jolley. And I must give a special thanks to Rick Frishman of Planned Television Arts for telling so many people about this guy named Willie Jolley; and for introducing me to Jeff Herman. You are the best!

I thank all of my speaker friends who have been so supportive and have "schooled me" on the publishing industry—Greg Godek, Mark Victor Hanson, Jack Canfield, Harvey Mackay, Dennis Kimbro, Charlie "Tremendous" Jones, Dave and David Yoho, George Fraser, Iyanla Van Zant, and of course my buddy and mentor, Les Brown. And thank you to all my friends in the National Speakers Association, who taught me about the speaking industry and about the power of giving and sharing. Also thanks to everyone at NSA who went to bookstores and made sure my books were "face out" and kept telling people "buy that Willie Jolley book!". I could not have done it without you. You are the best friends in the world!

Finally, I thank all the radio and television stations who interviewed me and allowed me to share my messages with the world; plus all the media outlets that wrote stories and publicized my books, music, and message. And I am so grateful for all the people who have come out to see me across the country. All the people at my speeches, all the corporate groups I visited, all the students in the schools where I spoke, all my Blessed and Highly Favored Club folks, and everyone who has bought my books and tapes. I appreciate each and every one of you. And thank you to those who have stopped me in the streets, written, or E-mailed me and let me know that my words or songs made a difference. That's why I do what I do. Your encouragement was the fuel that kept the fires burning. Thank you all and may God continue to bless you and keep you. I love you madly!

In every life there comes a time

A minute when you must decide

To stand up and live your dreams

Or fall back and live your fears.

In that minute of decision,

You must grasp the vision

And seize the power

that lies deep inside of you!

Then you will see

That dreams really can and do come true

And that all things truly are possible . . .

If you can just believe!

It only takes a minute to change your life!

It's time to turn your Setbacks into

Setups for Comebacks!

—Willie Jolley

Contents

A Setback Is a Setup for a Comeback!

I have only just a minute,

Only sixty seconds in it

Forced upon me can't refuse it,

Didn't seek it, Didn't choose it

But it's up to me to use it

I must suffer if I lose it

Give account if you abuse it

Just a tiny little minute

But an eternity is in it!

—Dr. Benjamin Mays

Foreword

*The minute you make a decision and take action . . .
is the minute you change your life!*

—Willie Jolley

The Starting Point

◇ ◇ ◇ It was a beautiful Saturday night in the fall of 1989. I was on my way to my nightly performance at The Newsroom Café, where I was the featured performer. I was feeling fantastic. I had just won my third WAMMIE (Washington DC version of a Grammy) for Best Jazz Singer and I knew that both shows that night were sold out. And it turned out to be a great night with two wonderful audiences. Later that evening, I was excited when I got the message that the club owner wanted to see me.

I didn't delay because after a night like this I could see a raise and contract extension coming my way. We sat down and he said "You were great tonight! The audiences loved you, and you've been doing really well lately. You've just won the awards for best jazz singer and best performer and all that. You've done everything we asked, which is why this is difficult. We've decided to make a change. We like you, and we like your band, but we decided to cut costs, you know downsize, right-size, human re-engineer." (You can call it what you want, it still means the same thing . . . FIRED.)

"So we decided to try this new thing that is catching on at other clubs. It's called a karaoke machine! We want to try that for about a month."

"A month?" I said, "What about my bills?" (I learned that night that nobody cares about your bills, but you and the people you owe!)

I was shocked. I was hurt. I was flabbergasted. I was devastated! I couldn't believe it, I had worked so hard to build up the clientele for the club, and I was being rewarded by getting fired and replaced by a karaoke machine. I had heard about other people losing their jobs, but I never expected it to happen to me. It was a setback! A Major Setback! Yet, at that same moment, it was also the start of a marvelous comeback. A comeback that has taught me, that a setback is really nothing but a setup for a comeback.

The Turning Point

From that moment I started changing my life. I went home and told my wife that I was sick and tired of someone telling me what to sing, what not to sing, when to sing, when not to sing. I was sick and tired of someone else controlling my destiny. The time had come; I was going to change my life.

I got on the phone and called my band and told them what had happened and that I had decided to go in another directions. They wished me luck, but luck was not what I was betting on; I was betting on me! I wasn't sure exactly what I was going to do but I was sure that I was going to change my life and I knew luck was not the deciding factor . . . I was.

I had read that "the real definition of luck is when preparation meets opportunity" and "if you don't have an opportunity then make one." I was tired of thinking like a musician, always "waiting for my break," waiting for someone to discover me and make me a star. I decided to change my thinking, change my actions and change my results. To stop "waiting for breaks" and start "making my breaks."

I remembered a quote I read about luck by Lucille Ball, after she had had a setback early in her career when she had been fired by a movie studio. A studio executive fired her because he felt she was "a no-talent actress." It was from that setback that she borrowed some money and created her own show. It was named "I Love Lucy" and it became a hit! In fact, it became the number one television show that year, and the next year, and the next year and the next year. The show went on to become the biggest syndicated show ever, and she went on to become one of the greatest comedic actresses of all time. Lucille Ball had a famous quote about luck, which states, "I have found it to be true, that the harder I work, the luckier I get." I couldn't agree more.

I bought into this new concept of making my breaks rather than waiting for them. I took a job with a junior college as a counselor. My job was to talk to students who were not doing well in school, and convince them to stay in school. It was there that I started learning about the power of motivation. When the semester was over I was offered a job with the Washington DC Public Schools as a drug prevention coordinator, talking to kids about staying away from drugs and alcohol. I started speaking and found that people truly seemed to be inspired and motivated by my speeches.

From speaking to kids in schools, the teachers and principals started inviting me to speak at their association meetings. From the associations meetings I got invitations to speak to other community groups. Those invitations brought forth additional invitations to speak at their churches. In the church congregations there were people who worked for major corporations, who invited me to come to their corporations. Then from there the people at the corporations told their friends at other companies about me and it started to grow.

Then Les Brown, The Motivator, heard me speak and sing at a program in Washington DC and asked me if I would like to be a part of a new tour he was starting with Gladys Knight called the Motivation and Music Tour. He liked the fact that I did both motivation and music and he felt I would be a great opener for them. From there I started touring with Les and Gladys and more opportunities came. From public speaking came radio and television, then books and records then tours and concerts.

Just think . . . I could still be singing in a smoky, little night-club if I hadn't been fired and replaced by a karaoke machine. In fact, sometimes I want to go back and hug that guy who fired me. He helped me learn firsthand, that a setback is nothing but a setup for a comeback!

Setbacks

Have you ever had a setback? Have you ever had a problem that knocked you down? Have you ever had a situation in your life that was painful? Have you ever been disappointed? Have you ever been heartbroken? Have you ever lost something, or someone, and could not seem to get your equilibrium back? Have you ever had a dilemma where the rug was pulled out from under you and you just didn't know what to do? Well if the answer is yes to these questions, this book will be of help to you.

This book is a "how-to" manual to turn your setbacks into comebacks. How to win in the face of opposition and adversity. How to turn life's lemons into lemonade, your scars into stars and your pain into power.

Have you ever wondered why some people can make a million dollars then lose it, make a second million, lose that, then make a third million, while others can't even make ends meet? Why is it that some people, no matter what they touch, it seems to turn to gold? Why is it? Well they know the formula, the recipe for success, and therefore can re-create success over and over again. They have adversities, they have setbacks, but they know the formula and can consistently turn those setbacks into comebacks. This book is designed to give you the recipe for effectively turning your problems into possibilities, turning your obstacles into opportunities, and turning your setbacks into comebacks.

It is also about the power of defining moments that change our lives and how we can make the most of those moments. It's not just about the power of the comeback, but also the power of the process, because there is power in the process.

In this book you will discover the excitement that is created when we turn setbacks, those moments of challenge and change, into minutes of victory. We will find how to grasp victory from the jaws of defeat and hope from desperate situations. When you have seen that it can be done, shown how it has been done and told "how" to do it, then you too can turn those challenging times into victorious times, turn your obstacles into opportunities, and turn your setbacks into comebacks.

The VDAD formula

This book is divided into four parts. A four-part formula for turning any setback into a comeback. The four-point formula is called the VDAD Formula and consists of:

1. The Power of Vision
2. The Power of Decision
3. The Power of Action
4. The Power of Desire

I have found this formula to be consistent in turning setbacks into comebacks. Just as other formulas consistently work, so does this—for example, when you take two parts hydrogen and mix it with one part oxygen you get water: likewise, when you take vision and add decision, action and desire you can, and will, turn your setbacks into comebacks.

Within the four-part VDAD Formula there are nine chapter steps or TIPS (which stands for techniques, ideas, principles, and strategies for success). The chapters are designed to give you ideas about how others have turned their setbacks into comebacks and how you can do the same. Ideas, plus examples and stories that detail how to turn your setbacks into comebacks. Stories of the famous and the not so famous, but stories of people who got extraordinary results, by using specific tools and techniques that turned their lives around. Techniques that you too can employ to turn your setbacks into comebacks.

The nine steps give you a specific step-by-step, point-by-point game plan, that will effectively guide you through the process to turn your setbacks into comebacks. And the nine steps work, no matter what the setback is.

The steps are:

1. Perspective—How do you see it? Is it a setback or is it a setup for a comeback?
2. Recognize it's Life—Don't take it personally
3. Focus on the Goal—If the dream is big enough the problems don't matter!
4. Make decisions—You've had a setback, Now what are you going to do about it?
5. Don't panic! Decide to stay calm, stay collected and stay positive!
6. Take action—persistent, determined action
7. Take responsibility—Face it, trace it, erase it, replace it

8. Have faith! You are blessed and highly favored!

9. Remember It's All Good! Be thankful, have an attitude of gratitude!

In each chapter I will give you some specifics points that are called "Teach Points." These are important nuggets that give us "A-Ha's" and specific information that can make a difference in our comebacks. I have found that life often gives us "Teach Points" but we do not see them in the midst of all the activities and information we are bombarded with. The same is true in this book; there is a lot of information and a lot of things that can get your attention, but I do not want you to miss these specific points. They have had such a positive impact on me that I felt it was important to highlight them for you. Plus there might be some other points you have seen that reach you and move you so I have included space at the end of each chapter for notes and your own "A-ha's".

In writing this book I have a few specific objectives. My first objective is to inspire people, because we all need inspiration. Many people think the word inspiration means "that which is religious," but that is not exactly correct. Most religious information is inspirational, but inspirational information does not specifically have to be religious. Let's first define inspire.

To inspire means to "breathe anew." Case in point, if you heard a news report that stated that John Doe expired at 10:02 am, you would know that the breath of life went out of him at 10:02. Well, inspire is the opposite of expire, it means that the breath of life is restored. It means to "breathe anew" into others. We have found that many people are discouraged and dejected, depressed and despondent because life has just beat them up so much that they feel defeated. Yet when they are inspired, there is a new vitality, a new energy, that is instilled in them.

We all need inspiration at some time or the other. I believe we should always look for inspiration. If we look we will usually find it. Some find it in music, or in paintings, or in looking at a beautiful scene, like a sunset. Wherever we find it we should constantly seek inspiration because in it we find renewal and refreshing.

Author and speaker Wayne Dyer says that you should try to be renewed daily, just as you cleanse and renew your outer self (your body) daily. You should also wash, feed and renew your inner self daily. You must make inspiration a part of your daily routine; otherwise your spiritual self goes lacking and can become disjointed.

Think about what happens to most people when they wake up in the morning; they turn on the television and hear about all the murders, and fires, and earthquakes, and tragedies, and how bad the economy is (even when it is doing good, some people are forecasting doom). And that is how they start their day. No, you need inspiration.

I know how important inspiration is to me. I make it a part of my daily routine to read and listen to positive, inspirational information. When I wake up I take time to pray and meditate, and read or listen to something positive, because statistics show that if you read or listen to something positive in the first twenty minutes of your day then your productivity will go up dramatically. Why is that?

If you woke up this morning and it was rainy and cold and wet and clammy outside, what does your body usually want to do? That's right, Go back to bed! Yet if you wake up and the sun is shining and the birds are singing and it's a beautiful day, you are more apt to want to get up and take advantage of that day, so as not to miss one minute.

The same is true for your psyche. If you wake up and hear how bad things are and how many negative things happened overnight, it creates a cloud above you and you might get up but you are not enthusiastic about jumping into that day. But if you wake up and read something positive like "The Lion and Gazelle" which states:

> *Every morning in Africa a gazelle wakes up*
> *And knows that it must run faster than the fastest lion*
> *Or it will be killed and eaten.*
> *Also every morning in Africa a lion wakes up*
> *And knows that it must outrun the slowest gazelle*
> *Or it will starve to death.*
> *It doesn't matter whether you are a lion or a gazelle . . .*
> *When the sun comes up, you'd better be running.*

Or you could wake up, read some scripture and shout out something like this scriptural text, "This is the day, which the Lord has made, let us rejoice and be glad in it!"

Whatever you do, make it a habit to wake up and start your day with that which is positive, powerful and inspirational. When you start your day in a positive way you begin your day with a new perspective, a new attitude and a new excitement. You are excited about being alive, and if you are excited about being alive, you are more apt to try more. If you try more, you are more apt to achieve more. Choose to program yourself, rather than letting the negative naysayers program you. Choose to win!

When you are inspired you can then share inspiration with your friends and families. For many years, when I was singing for a living, I was not interested in inspiring people, I just wanted to impress them. I would sing loud and strong and listen to the audience "Ooh and Ahh" and I was happy because they were impressed. But when I became a speaker I went through some real challenging times, some difficult and painful times, that helped me to realize that I was here not just to impress but, more importantly, to inspire. Once I changed my focus and made a commitment to inspiring, not impressing, wonderful things started to happen in my life and in my career. I learned about service and sharing. Cavett Robert, the great dean of motivational speakers said, "Service is the rent we pay for the space we occupy on earth!" Jim Rhon, the great motivational philosopher says, "Service to many is the path that leads to greatness." Finally Jesus Christ, the carpenter from Galilee, taught that those who are the greatest will be those who are the servants of many. Service, and sharing inspiration, are much more important than being served and impressing others.

Next I want to give information. "Information is power" is how the saying goes. In order to really have power and make a difference you must have some "how to's," which are specific ways on how to use the information. If I share the information and the how to's with you, as others have shared with me, and you in turn share the information with others, who then also share it with more people, then we can create a network of people who are not afraid of setbacks. They will have a good understanding and confidence that they will grow from the setbacks and use them to propel them to future success. The key is that we must be willing to share the information (and you cannot share what you do not have, and cannot show what you do not know). This is why I feel it is important to share what I have learned from my failures as well as my successes, my pain as well as my joy.

When I was just starting in the music business I went to hear a great blues singer named Mary Jefferson. She was incredible! After her performance I told her I was a jazz singer but I also wanted to learn how to sing the blues, like she sang them. She smiled and said, "Baby, I can teach you the notes and the words, but that won't make you a blues singer. See baby, you've got to suffer to sing the blues!"

I have always remembered that lesson. I realized that it is nice for people to hear about my accomplishments, but it is more powerful to hear about my struggles, and what I did to overcome them. We can be of service telling our successes, but can be of greater service telling about our pains, and how we made it through the storms of life.

Finally I wanted to share my personal philosophy in this book, which includes my theological perspectives. After graduating from college I had a great "desire to inspire" and so I figured I would go to a theological seminary, since the only people I knew who dealt with inspiration were preachers. But after going for three years and getting a degree I realized I had not heard the call to preach. It was so bewildering. I knew I had this desire to inspire but I had not heard the call to preach. I didn't know what to do.

It was a very painful time because no one, including myself, could understand why I had gone through all the years of college and seminary and not become a preacher. I graduated from seminary and was offered a church, but I couldn't accept it because I believed that a preacher is a high calling of God and should not be entered into frivolously. If I didn't hear the call I knew I couldn't take on that office, so I pursued my other love, entertaining.

I became a jingle singer and nightclub performer (quite a change, huh?) and had some success in the music business. I sang jingles for lots of commercial and was awarded five consecutive Washington Area Music Awards. Three for "Best Male Jazz Vocalist" and two for "Best Inspirational Male Vocalist." I performed to standing room only audiences every night and had quite a bit of success. Until I had my karaoke setback. A setback that changed my life and helped me to find my destiny!

It was after that setback that I took a job with the Washington DC Public Schools as a drug prevention coordinator and started speaking to kids about staying away from drugs. It was during that year that I found my "speaking voice" and discovered an ability to mix motivation, inspiration and entertainment. From there I created a concept called "InspirTainment" and took InspirTainment to kids, then to colleges and corporations, then to people across America and then across the globe. This book will share some of my InspirTainment philosophy, some inspiration, some motivation, some of my theological ideas and I hope it will also be entertaining in the process.

I also want to make it clear that I will talk about my faith because I believe faith is an important ingredient in success and in overcoming challenges. I remember when my first book came out a lawyer friend said, "I like your book, but I am a little confused. I thought this was a success book, and then I read about how you kept talking about God in your book. I don't understand what God has to do with success." I wrote back, "It is a success book, and therefore I have shared my philosophy on success, and I believe that my faith and my success are inseparable. I cannot have one without the other. It is like trying to separate the wet from the water, the hot from the fire. My faith and my success cannot be separated!"

Throughout the book I will share tidbits and nuggets that I have found in the Bible that deal directly with success and overcoming obstacles. I truly believe that the Bible is one of the greatest success manuals ever written. It gives incredible success strategies and techniques and a formula for success as well as a formula for turning your setbacks into powerful comebacks. Plus, according to a Gallup Poll, it is the number one most read and bestselling book of all times. According to a recent study in *USA Today*, it is a source of inspiration and information for most of today's major success stories. I have found many answers about setbacks in the Bible and it has given wonderful examples of how to turn setbacks into comebacks.

So in short this book is about problem solving, creative thinking, motivation, leadership and faith. If you can grasp these concepts you can turn your setbacks into comebacks.

So "Tally ho, Let's go" . . . It's time to turn some setbacks into comebacks!

Introduction

··

It Only Takes a Minute . . .
to Turn a Setback into a Comeback!

◇ ◇ ◇ I was talking with my friend, bestselling author Dennis Kimbro, about how sad it is to see people who have had setbacks, get knocked down and just give up. During that conversation Dennis said, "Willie we've got to help people see that a setback is not the end of the road, it's like a comeback waiting to happen!"

"You're right. It's like a setup for the comeback."

"Yeah!"

"Yeah! Wow! That's it, Dennis, . . . a setback, is really a setup for a comeback"

I believe that you must get a new way of thinking about setbacks. We need to see a setback as a thing to be embraced rather than a thing to be rejected, because if there were no setbacks, then there could be no comebacks. If you want to have a comeback, then you must come back from something; in other words, setbacks are prerequisites for comebacks. Adversity is also a part of the equation. Adversity and challenges are life's way of creating strength. Adversity creates challenge, and challenge creates change, and change is absolutely necessary for growth. If there is no change and challenge, there can be no growth and development.

Yet most people dread adversity and change. Someone told me that the only thing that likes change is a wet baby, but change is absolutely necessary for growth. Successful people not only embrace change but they do all they can to create it and drive it! They understand that change is a necessary part of success, and in order to grow, you must be willing to change.

Change is a necessary part of life, and a necessary part of our existence. Yet change is uncomfortable. We all get used to things a certain way and when they change we have to rearrange and readjust, and that is uncomfortable. As we go from childhood to being a teenager, we go through uncomfortable changes. As we go from being a teenager to a young adult, we go through uncomfortable changes. In each stage of life we continually go through changes and they are uncomfortable. That is why we call them growing pains.

We might experience change in our careers, by getting a new job, which means we must make new adjustments. Or we might lose a job, or have a job reversal or get passed by on the job of our dreams. It will be uncomfortable. We might experience change in our relationships, with a breakup or divorce or the death of a loved one. We might experience a change in our personal lives, with our finances or our health or with our family and friends. Change can come in a number of ways and most of them are uncomfortable, yet they happen and we must grow from them. In fact change is absolutely necessary for growth. And setbacks are part of the change/growth process.

Anyone who has had any measure of success has had a setback. Whether it is Thomas Edison, Walt Disney, George Washington Carver, Michael Jordan, Steven Spielberg, Oprah Winfrey or any other successful person. They all have had setbacks. The common elements are Vision (a big dream); Decision (a willingness to make tough decisions); Action (definitive action on the dream); and Desire (a commitment to keep going until you reach your goal).

One of my favorites is Dr. Seuss, who was turned down by just about every publisher in the country. Only one publisher believed in him, but that was all he needed, and he went on to have massive success.

Friends, setbacks are a part of success, a major part of success, and setbacks are nothing but comebacks waiting to happen.

What Is a Setback? (and What It Is Not!)

Webster's defines *setback* as "a checking of progress, an unexpected reverse or defeat, a hindrance, a check, a reversal, an impediment, a block, an obstruction, a defeat, a delay, a disadvantage, a disappointment, a hold-up, a rebuff, an upset, a loss or a relapse." Did you notice the words "Death" "The End" or "Finish" do not appear in this group? This shows that a setback is not the end! As author John Capozzi says, "A turn, or bend in the road, is not the end of the road . . . unless you fail to make the turn!"

In reality, it is not the end. It is a temporary situation that can be turned around. It is not death! Death is death, and a setback is a setback. They are not the same.

There might be times when people have setbacks and they may appear dead. They may be on the verge of death or on the verge of giving up and calling it a done deal, but as long as there is a small spark left, there is the possibility for turning it around and coming back.

Tina Turner is a wonderful example. After years of abuse from her husband she finally decided to leave. She disappeared from the public view and tried to get a record contract in

America, but was turned down by numerous companies and told she was washed up. But Tina Turner disagreed and made up her mind that she was going to come back stronger than ever. She went to Europe and recorded a song called "Let's Stay Together," which became a hit. She then came back to America and recorded an album called "What's Love Got To Do With It," which became a massive success. She has gone on to become one of the highest grossing female concert artists in the world. She proved that a setback is nothing but a setup for a comeback.

John Travolta is another example of a comeback kid in action. After a successful run on the television show "Welcome Back Mr. Kotter" he drifted on to do a few more shows, which were not successful. Then he appeared in a few "B" movies which were also not successful, and he just disappeared from the scene. Many thought he was done, finished, through, but *he* didn't. He decided to come back and started with a movie called *Pulp Fiction*. The movie was a hit and he continued to have one hit after another. He has gone on to become one of the highest paid actors in Hollywood. A setback is nothing but a setup for a comeback.

Lee Iocooca was fired from Ford and left for dead. The only job he could get was with Chrysler Motors, which was on the verge of bankruptcy. Yet Iococca turned his setback into an incredible comeback where he not only transformed himself but he also revived and transformed Chrysler.

Lee Iococca, John Travolta and Tina Turner understood that like the Phoenix, who rises out of the ashes, as long as there is an ember, a spark of life, you can come back.

Now let's look at the word *comeback*. Webster's defines a comeback as "a return to a former position or condition; recovery, rebound, rebuttal, reply, respond, revive, retort." The key is to learn how to change your patterns and responses to consistently turn your setbacks into setups for comebacks.

We must learn to see adversity as strength developers and setbacks as comeback creators.

Adversity

While prosperity best discovers vice, adversity best discovers virtue, and the virtue that comes from adversity is fortitude. The good things, which belong to prosperity, are to be wished, but the good things, which belong to adversity, are to be admired. Therefore he knows not of his own strength that has not met adversity.

—Sir Francis Bacon

If we had no winter, the spring would not be so pleasant. If we had no adversity, then prosperity would not be so welcome.

—Anne Bradstreet

Adversity can either break you or make you. The same hammer that breaks the glass, also sharpens the steel.

—Bob Johnson, President of
Black Entertainment Television

Good timber does not grow with ease; the stronger the wind, the stronger the trees.

—J. Willard Marriott

If thou faint in the time of adversity, thou strength is small.

—Proverbs 24:10

Anyone who is moving ahead in life is always going to have setbacks. The only ones who don't are the people who are dead or have just given up. As long as you are alive and getting up and trying to do something with your life, you will have setbacks. Ultimately the difference between Winners and Losers and the key to long-term success, is not talent or ability, chances or lucky breaks, but it is the way you view and handle setbacks and adversity. There are other things that might play a part, but the key to success will be how you handle setbacks, because sooner or later everyone has them. Losers see setbacks as the end of the road, while winners see setbacks as a bend in the road. This ultimately makes the difference between those who win and those who lose.

> *Far better to dare mighty things, to win glorious triumphs, even though checkered by failure, than to take rank with poor spirits who neither enjoy much nor suffer much, because they live in the gray twilight that knows not victory or defeat. The joy of living is his who has the heart to demand it.*
>
> —Theodore Roosevelt

In his book *Adversity Quotient*, Dr. Paul Stoltz says that there are three measure quotients, or standard predictors, that impact our success. There is IQ, Intelligence Quotient, EQ, Emotional Quotient, and AQ, Adversity Quotient. For many years most scientists and educators believed that IQ was the main predictor of success. They felt that if you had a high IQ then you were automatically destined for success. Then came Ted Kaczynski, the "Unabomber," who was a genius, but had no social skills and could not handle the pressures of life, so he became a mad bomber.

We all have seen intelligent people who have misused their intelligence and therefore never reached their potential, or who couldn't handle life's challenges and gave up, some even end up on the street begging for handouts. Intelligence alone does not guarantee success.

Daniel Goldman wrote in his book, *Emotional Intelligence*, that intelligence is not enough to guarantee success, you must have high EQ. Goldman defines EQ as that hypothetical measurement that reflects one's ability to work and empathize with others, control impulses, make good decision and have high self-esteem. He states that you can be smart in more than one way. People with high EQ tend to excel in real life with relationships, job performance and promotions and with community activities. Goldman shows that many people with high IQs fail, while their counterparts with moderate IQs succeed. In other words, IQ may help you get the job, but EQ will help you keep and excel in the job.

Adversity Quotient on the other hand is the newest predictor of success and it is a concept that states that IQ is great, and EQ is wonderful, but the real determination of success is AQ, which is how you handle adversity. Stoltz says that everyone is born with a basic human drive to grow and ascend, like going up a mountain. As we go up the mountain we will notice that achievement is not uniform; there will be fewer people (and companies) at the top than at the bottom. He says the reason is because of AQ.

AQ is the level of adversity that one is conditioned to go through to ascend the mountain and reach one's goals. He says there are three groups and three levels of AQ. First are "The Quitters," who are the people who abandon the climb when times get tough and simply give up. The second group is called "The Campers." These are the people who start going up the mountain and get to a smooth spot and camp out there, and end up staying there. Campers tend to see change as a problem, rather than an opportunity.

The final group is called "The Climbers." Climbers are people who are committed to reach their goals and are committed to living their dreams and being all they can be. They understand success is not a destination, it is a journey . . . a process. They might get knocked down as they move along the path, but they keep getting up and they keep going up, climbing higher and higher. Climbers are positive thinkers as well as positive doers. They keep going in spite of the obstacles. Climbers see obstacles and setbacks as a nuisance, yet as a natural part of the process. They are willing to face the problems in order to reach their goal. Campers and climbers must meet at the same place during challenging times. Campers see camp as home, while climbers see camp as a base camp, a temporary place from which to continue the climb.

Stoltz says campers who stay at the camp too long, will begin to atrophy and lose their ability to climb and get slower and weaker all the time. Climbers, on the other hand, get stronger and stronger as they continue to climb. They grow from their challenges and realize that adversity really does create strength. They cultivate their strength by way of their willingness to climb in the midst of adversity and therefore tend to be excellent leaders, like Mohandas Gandhi, Martin Luther King, Jr., Winston Churchill, Franklin D. Roosevelt, and Nelson Mandela. Climbers are people who are willing to climb and fight, despite the obstacles.

In the book *The Courage to Fail*, author Art Mortell speaks about the fact that we learn more from failure than from success. Mr. Mortell shares how all successful people realize that failure is a part of success. He writes, "Without adversity there is no growth. Adversity challenges and pushes us to accelerate the development of our greatest potential. Adversity and failure can actually become the catalyst for success." We must be willing to go through, and grow through the challenges. We must be willing to struggle, in order to really succeed!

Flight . . . Is in the Struggle!

There was a little boy walking through the forest and he came upon a cocoon of an emperor moth. He took it home so that he could watch the moth come out of the cocoon. He sat and watched for several hours as the moth struggled to force its body through the little hole. It struggled and struggled and seemed to be having a very difficult time. The little boy decides to make it easy for the butterfly so he takes out his pocketknife and cuts a slit in the cocoon to allow the little butterfly to get out and help it to fly. When the butterfly appeared it did not look like a regular butterfly. It had a swollen body and small shriveled wings.

The little boy was upset and confused so he ran and got his grandfather to come see the strange-looking butterfly. He told his grandfather how he had tried to make it easy for the struggling butterfly by cutting a hole in the cocoon, and how he came out and wasn't able to fly. The wise grandfather took the boy by the hand and explained that when the moth is struggling to get through the tiny hole it is really forcing the fluid from the body into the wings. Without the struggle the wings could not grow. Without the struggle the butterfly's wings would never be strong enough to fly, and without flight the butterfly probably would not be able to survive. Friends, the moral of the story is that flight and life are in the struggle. Without challenge and struggles we would never grow and never reach our fullest potential. Life really is in the struggle!

I was out early one morning for my morning run and jogged by an older gentleman whom I had seen before. I said "Good morning" and he replied the same. He asked how I was doing and I said, "This early morning exercise is a struggle" and he replied, "Yes it is, but everything good comes with struggle!"

As I ran on, I said to myself, "That is very true! Everything good that I have ever had, came with some degree of struggle. I had to struggle to get a record contract in my teens. I had to struggle through college by singing jingles and in nightclubs. When I started speaking I had to struggle to start my company. I had to struggle to build my company. I have had different types of struggle, but every achievement was the result of struggle!"

Nido Qubein, the great speaker, author and philanthropist, says, "Abundance grows out of adversity and struggle."

The same is true for us, we need challenge in order to grow. We live in a time when people are exercising and working out like never before. Gym membership and attendance continues to increase. Those who are into weight lifting and bodybuilding know that there is a definite correlation between the size of the weight and the size and strength of the muscle; the heavier the weight the bigger the muscle. The same is true for adversity. Little challenges create little muscles, while big challenges create big muscles. We must be willing to face adversity in order to grow.

Part I

The Power
of Vision

Step 1

....

Perspective: Check Your Vision . . . What Do You See? Because What You See Is What You Get!

Is there anything worse than blindness? Yes!
Eyesight . . . but no vision!

—Helen Keller

Man is only limited by the audacity of his
imagination!

—Autere

Where there is no vision, the people perish.

—Proverbs 29:10

Vision!

Mediocrity is a place and it is bordered on the north
by compromise, on the south by indecision, on the east
by past thinking, and on the west by lack of vision.

John Mason

◇ ◇ ◇ The starting point of success, the starting point of changing your life and the starting point of turning your setbacks into setups for comebacks is vision. In order to turn your setback into a setup for a comeback you must have vision! You must have a goal and you must stay focused on the goal. Vision is the first step in the quest to turn your setback into a setup for a comeback. First let's make sure we understand what vision is.

Vision, is an image of what's possible for your life and your perspective or way of looking at life. If you have a vision for your life then you have a view of the destination for our life and a view of what you're after. Scripture says, "Where there is no vision the people perish." What goes unsaid is "Where there is a vision the people will perish!" You must have a vision in your life in order to turn your setbacks into setups for comebacks.

It is important to define the word *vision*. First, many people believe that vision means eyesight. Do you need eyesight to turn a setback into a setup for a comeback? The answer is NO! Helen Keller proved that. She was blind and deaf, yet she became one of the greatest women of all times. Stevie Wonder proved that you do not need eyesight to become great. He grew up blind and poor in Saginaw, Michigan, but he had a vision to become great and he kept trying and trying until he was discovered and signed by Motown Records. Stevie Wonder has gone on to be one of the most prolific musicians of this century. Ray Charles also had a setback as a child, when he started losing his sight at the age of five. His mother didn't have the money to take him to a specialist and he eventually went blind. He could have given up but he decided to fight for his dream. He went on to become an American icon.

Jose Feliciano was born poor, and blind in Puerto Rico. Some of the neighbors suggested that he get a cup and beg for money like blind people were supposed to do, but Jose refused! He found an "old piece of guitar" and taught himself how to play. He practiced day and night, night and day, sometimes until his fingers bled. Today Jose Feliciano is considered one of the greatest guitarists of all time. He wrote a song we sing every Christmas called "Felis Navidad". You don't need eyesight to turn a setback into a setup for a comeback.

The first type of vision is eyesight, the next type is hindsight, which is being able to look back at past events. Is hindsight necessary to turn a setback into a setup for a comeback? No! It's good to have hindsight, so you do not repeat the mistakes of the past, but unfortunately most people who start dealing with the past get stuck! They think in the past, dwell in the past, live in the past. They cannot get past the past! They dwell on what people said to them ten years ago or what happened to them as children and cannot get past it. I say, *The past is supposed to be a place of reference, not a place of residence! There is a reason why your car has a big windshield and a small rearview mirror. You are supposed to keep your eyes on where you are going, and just occasionally check out where you have been . . . Otherwise you are going to crash!*

I love this quote about life. "*The difference between life and school is that in school you get the lesson and then you get the test. In life you get the test and then you get the lesson."* Without a test there can be no testimony. As Kierkegaard, the German philosopher, said, *"Life is often understood backwards but must be lived forward."* Learn from the past but don't dwell there.

The first type of vision is eyesight, then there is hindsight and the next type of vision is insight! Insight is the power to see inside a situation, and get to the inner nature of things. It is that "still small voice within us." Some call it intuition, which means inner teacher, and others call it perspective. I see insight as being a combination of your experiences, logic, perspective and sensitivity to your inner voice as well as to a higher voice guiding you from within. Unfortunately most people have turned the volume down. They do not listen to the voice within. They listen to all the cynics and negative people on the outside. Sometimes we need to remind ourselves of our victories and stop looking at our failures. Listen to the small voice within that says "Look, you have had some successes and have even greater things yet to come. If you did it then you can do it now. Just try! You can do it!" Turn up the volume on your inner voice and realize you can do incredible things if you just try.

The last kind of sight is *foresight*! Foresight is the ability to see into the future, not as a fortune teller does, but as a person who is creating what they see in their mind. Foresight is about destination and determination. It is the sight that allows you to see down the road and believe what you see is possible. Scripture says that foresight is connected to faith where you can "call forth those things that be not, as if they were". Foresight, mixed with insight, creates a powerful force called a dream; and dreams are the seeds for success. You must be willing to dream and believe that the dream is possible, no matter how many others say it is impossible. Insight and foresight mixed together are the keys to tapping into the power of vision and are the keys to starting on the comeback trail.

Perspective

Every crucial experience can be regarded either as a setback, or the start of wonderful new adventure, it depends on your perspective!
—Mary Roberts Rinehart

We will sometimes have defeats in life but you can have defeats without being defeated, you can fail without being a failure. Winners see failure and defeats as merely part of the process to get to win.
—Maya Angelou

Perspective is an important part of the vision concept. Perspective means how do you view the situation? How do you see it? Do you see this as a problem or do you see this as an opportunity? Do you see it as a change or as a chance?

Do you see it as a new beginning or as the end? Do you see it as an entrance or as an exit? Do you see it as the end of the road or as a bump in the road? Do you see it as a setback "period" or do you see it as a setback "comma?" In other words, do you see it as the end of the sentence, or do you see it as just a break in the sentence, a slight pause? Do you see it as a setback, or as a setup for a comeback? This is a very important question that will greatly impact how you will respond.

First, is the glass half empty or is the glass half full? Is the night ending or is the day beginning. Whatever perspective you choose will have a major impact on the decisions you will make. The decisions you make will determine the actions that you will take. Then the actions you take will determine the results you create.

Some people manage to use adversity as a motivational force, which helps to strengthen them, while others allow adversity to crush and limit them. The key is how you view adversity. You must decide to have and maintain a positive perspective. Your uplook determines your outlook, and your outlook determines your outcome, and that is when you start to realize that "Yes, you know I really think I can make a comeback."

Wherever you find a crisis you will also always find an opportunity. Napoleon Hill, the author of the classic book *Think and Grow Rich*, wrote: "Every adversity contains, at the same time, a seed of equivalent opportunity!" You must be willing to see that and then willing to take the steps to turn those adverse moments into exciting, life-defining moments. The key is *how* to turn those moments of adversity around so you too can snatch victory from the jaws of defeat.

If there were no problems there would be no opportunities! The old saying states that the key to success is to find a problem and solve it. Sometimes you don't even have to look for a problem, the problems finds you . . . you have a setback!

When you have a setback you also have a choice that you must make. Do you see it as a setback that you should cry about, or do you see it as an opportunity that you should be excited about? It truly is your choice. The old success adage says, "The key to success is to find a need and fill it. Find a problem and solve it." Wherever there are problems there are also opportunities! If there were no problems there would be no opportunities.

Even with the challenges of life, I still say that the good greatly outweighs the bad, the happy outweighs the sad, and the pleasure outweighs the pain, but it depends on how you choose to see it. From what perspective do you choose to view it? Do you see it from a positive perspective or a negative perspective? Life is challenging, but it is also a wonderful and beautiful adventure. From the minute you are born to the minute you die you will have some beauty and you will have challenges. Anyone who doesn't is either lying or dead! You must decide what you choose to focus on. Do you look for the good or do you look for the bad?

The Power of Perspective
A large shoe company sent two sales reps out to different parts of Australia to see if they could drum up some business from the Aborigines. One rep sent a message back saying, "Waste of time, no business here . . . Aborigines don't wear shoes." The other sent a message, "Send more troops, great business opportunity here, Aborigines don't wear shoes!" It all depends upon how you see the glass: is it half empty or half full? That is a question that you and only you can answer? And your perspective determines your answer. It is a positive perspective or is it a negative perspective.

Sometimes a setback will come in the form of an exit door. You will be forced to leave something or someone and it can be uncomfortable. It might be frightening and painful because

3. Develop resilience so you can bounce off and fly in a higher trajectory.
4. Break the law, Murphy's Law. Keep going forward.
5. You and God make a majority.
6. Have faith, focus, follow-through.
7. Don't be intimidated by the obstacles.
8. Learn new ways to win.
9. Don't take it personally. Exercise FIDO (forget it and drive on).
10. Sometimes you must break the law . . . Murphy's Law!

moral of the story is that most people would rather settle for known hells than unknown heavens.

I remember having obstacles in the past that looked like impassable mountains, but after I had overcome them they looked more like little molehills. I believe we all experience that if we are just willing to look back and look objectively. Think back to problems in your life, or maybe just life experiences that you had to go through. Like going through high school or college. It might have seemed like a big deal before you started but was a lot smaller after you finished.

I like this quote by Sidney J. Harris, "When I hear somebody sigh that "Life is hard," I am always tempted to ask, "Compared to what?" Yes, life is challenging but it is also filled with beautiful possibilities, it depends on your perspective. Look for the positive and realize that a setback is not the end of the road, but is just a bend in the road.

Step #1—Teaching Points

1. Without a vision a people will perish, but with a vision a people will flourish.
2. The past is supposed to be a place of reference, not a place of residence.
3. In school you get the lesson then the test, while in life you get the test then the lesson.
4. Life is to be understood backward, but must be lived forward.
5. We can have defeats without being defeated.
6. See it as a setback comma, rather than a setback period.
7. If there were no problems there would be no opportunities.
8. Every exit is also an entrance to a new place filled with new possibilities.

9. Do not settle for known hells when you can have unknown heavens.
10. If you search for good you will find it. Therefore decide to have a positive perspective.

Step 2

· ·

Recognize: It's Life! Don't Take It Personally! Sometimes You're the Windshield, Sometimes You're the Bug!

These are the times that try men's souls!
—Thomas Paine

◇ ◇ ◇ Yes, these are the times that try men's souls. These are also the times that try women's souls, and children's souls, and senior citizen souls. These are simply trying times. So were the days before you were born and so will be the days after you die. In other words, "LIFE IS TRYING!" Your parents had some trying times and your grandparents had some trying times and your great grandparents had trying times. And you are going to have trying times. Before we get going let's make sure this point is clear: life is challenging. It was challenging yesterday, it is challenging today, and it will be challenging tomorrow.

Every day you wake up, you will be faced with trying times. Every day you wake up you will face a new set of challenges. In the book *The Road Less Traveled*, the first line sums it up, "Life is difficult . . . period!" And it's true! Life is difficult, life is challenging, and it is hard. As long as you live you will have some challenges and some problem. Someone once said "In life either you have a problem, just left a problem, or you are on your way to a problem." That's life!

Let me make it clear that even though life is trying, it is also beautiful and wonderful and fantastic. It offers great possibilities and wonderful challenges, which is a good thing. Without challenges a baby would never learn to walk, and thereby to run. Without challenges we would never learn to read and to learn about new ideas. Without challenges we would never grow and stretch. Without challenges we would not have the tremendous technological advances that we have come to value as a major part of our lifestyles: light bulbs, cars, planes, computers, and television.

Life is about ups and downs, ins and outs, sunshine and rain. Hopefully you will have more ups than downs, ins than outs, and more sunny days than rainy days. Without rain there would be no rainbow and without the rain there would be no plants and food. With the challenges come strength and growth. *Life is about waves and waves are good. If you go into a hospital and the EKG gets a straight line . . . then you are dead.*

In every life there will be times of challenge and times of adversity, and I say that it is all good. Either those moments can mold you and make you or bust you and break you. Everybody, and I do mean EVERYBODY, will have problems and challenging times. And the rules emphatically state, "As long as you are alive you will have some pleasure and you will have some pain. You will have some sunshine and you will have some rain. You will have ups and you will have downs. You will have smiles and sometimes you will have frowns." That's it! It's Life 101: Sometimes you're the windshield sometimes you're the bug!

When you are the windshield you are big and strong and invincible and no problems. A beautiful morning, a beautiful day, a wonderful feeling, and everything is going your way! You are the king or the queen of the road! Watch out world here you come! When you're the bug, you will keep running into obstacles. You have one challenge after another, one windshield or brick wall after another, and one problem after another. But just because you have a day when you are the bug does not mean you have to lose! It depends on your attitude and perspective.

If you are the bug and you have a negative attitude and a negative perspective you see the setback as THE END! You hit a windshield, an obstacle, a problem, and WHAM you crash, are smashed and burn, you give up and it's over. Yet if you have a positive attitude and a positive perspective you see the setback as a minor daily occurrence, a part of life, a gnat in life's big ball field. When you have a positive attitude and a positive perspective you develop something called "bounce back ability" or "resiliency." When you hit the windshield you no longer smash and crash and die. You hit the windshield and then you bounce off, bounce up and fly! When you bounce off the windshield you are then thrust into a higher trajectory and you start to fly at a higher level!

Bounce back ability is a major part of turning your setbacks into setups for comebacks. Some call it bounce back ability and some call it resilience, which is the ability to recover and adjust to challenge and change. Whatever you call it, the key is that you quickly recover from the setback and refuse to let it keep you down. You don't crash, smash, burn and die. You bounce back and bounce up and fly. To turn your setbacks into comebacks, you must have bounce back ability; therefore you must be resilient.

The Rock 'Em, Sock 'Em Bolo Bag

When I was a child, my brother and I would constantly have boxing matches, which sometimes ended up with us getting battered and bruised. My parents got sick of the fights and decided to channel the energy in another direction, so they bought a Bolo Bag. The Bolo Bag was a plastic punching bag that had a weighted base and it had a silly face painted on the front. When inflated you could punch the bag as much as you wanted. The trick was that, due to the weighted base, the bag and the air-filled body the bag would always bounce back up.

My brother and I would punch on that bag for hours trying to knock it down and it would always bounce back up. No matter how hard we hit it, it kept popping back up. Our friends would come over and play with it and everyone was amazed how it would always bounce back. After a few weeks of hitting on the bag and not being able to get it to stay down we got tired and soon found some other toys to play with. We would occasionally come back and try to knock it down, but true to form, it would always bounce back.

Life is similar. Life comes along and knocks us down and tries to keep us down, but we must be like that Bolo Bag and keep bouncing back up. If we do, life will eventually get tired and frustrated and leave us alone for a while and go look for someone else. Now life will come back every once in a while and give us a quick shot and see if it can keep us down, but we should be like that Bolo Bag and keep bouncing back up.

Yet, the question remains. How do you bounce back? How do you become resilient? Like everything else in turning your setback into a comeback, you must decide! You must decide to have a positive attitude and decide to bounce back. I am not saying it will be easy, because it won't be. I recommend that you repeat this phrase whenever life knocks you down, "I might be down for a moment, but I am not out! I want to let the world know I shall bounce back and I am coming back!"

Murphy's Law!

We have all heard about Murphy's Law, which means anything that can go wrong will go wrong, at the worst possible time.

Murphy will come and visit everyone at some time or the other. Murphy is the king of setbacks. He creates setbacks and makes sure that everybody has some. Some get more than their share though, because they make Murphy feel at home and do not know how to make Murphy know that he is not welcome (one man recently told me that Murphy was presently living in the spare room of his house). Murphy can be counteracted; Murphy can be sent packing. How? By making it too uncomfortable for him to stay.

You can make it too uncomfortable for Murphy to stay by making his quest to disrupt your life too hard. You make it too hard by deterring him, making him work and making him look for an easier target. It's like the people who use an anti-theft device on their cars, if the thief wants the car badly enough they probably can get it. The device is a deterrent, it makes it harder and makes the thief think twice about it. The thief will think about whether they really want to work so hard for your car, when there is another car up the street that doesn't have an anti-theft device. You must develop a deterrent system for Murphy. The deterrent system for Murphy is called persistence, that's right . . . plain old persistence. You must just keep moving toward your goal, in spite of Murphy.

When Murphy stops by and throws you a curve ball you must persist. You must make a determined decision that you will simply not give up. The longer you persist, the weaker Murphy will get.

Step 2—Teaching Points

1. Life is trying, that is why you must continue to try.
2. Life is about waves and waves are good, on an EKG a straight line means you are dead.

3. Develop resilience so you can bounce off and fly in a higher trajectory.
4. Break the law, Murphy's Law. Keep going forward.
5. You and God make a majority.
6. Have faith, focus, follow-through.
7. Don't be intimidated by the obstacles.
8. Learn new ways to win.
9. Don't take it personally. Exercise FIDO (forget it and drive on).
10. Sometimes you must break the law . . . Murphy's Law!

Step 3

· ·

Focus On Your Goal! If the Dream Is Big Enough, The Problems Don't Matter!

Nothing ever built arose to touch the skies unless someone dreamed that it should, believed that it could and willed that it must!

All men dream, but not equally. Those men that dream at night in the dusty recesses of their minds, awaken to find that it was just vanity. But those that dream by day are the dangerous ones, for they dream with their eyes open, to make sure that their dreams will come true!

—T.E. Lawrence

◊ ◊ ◊ The next step to turning your setbacks into setups for comebacks is that you must focus your energies on the dream, on the vision, on your goal. You must have vision and you must have a goal, and you must realize that they are different. A goal is something you work on while a vision is something that works on you.

Sharks

In order to reach your goals and live your dreams, you must be motivated and there are two types of motivation: inspiration and desperation. Most people usually allow desperation to motivate them. They only get motivated when their backs are up against the wall and they have no other choice. Well, what would happen if they were motivated every day? The following poem says it best.

> *Most folks don't know how fast they can swim, until there are sharks pursuing them. But the one who succeeds in life's great race is the one who wisely sets the pace. Their pace is not set as fear requires, their stroke is a result of their desire. As you're faced with the ocean of decision, are you guided by fear or by vision? Have you set your goals? Are you trying to reach high marks? Or are you still waiting to see the sharks? Is it inspiration or desperation that you need to live your dreams. It's up to you!*
>
> —Author Unknown

A few years ago I had the opportunity to spend a day with multimillionaire and network marketing king, Dexter Yager. Dexter Yager is a former truck driver who built a multimillion dollar distribution network. It was one of the most intriguing days of my life. I learned a lot about success and a lot about overcoming failure.

Dexter shared story after story about the power of positive thinking and the power of adversity in growing you to the type of person you can be, if you are willing to dream and to fight for the dream. He also talked about setbacks and how to grow from them. During our conversation he said something I will never forget, he said, "As you go toward your dream you will have problems and difficulties, but if the dream is big enough . . . the problems don't matter!" I loved it! If the dream is big enough the problems don't count!

As time went on I read his book, *Don't Let Anybody Steal Your Dream*, and learned more about his philosophy on dreams and success. Here are some of Dexter Yager's classic quotes:

Some say, "It's hard, it's so hard!" That's right it is hard! And therefore you must go at it in a hard way. You must be willing to fight for your dream and fight hard for it, and realize that as you fight you will get stronger. You might get knocked down, but keep getting up and keep fighting. Those who refuse to lose, rarely do!

The paradox of life is that success is built on inconvenience, never convenience. Those who are willing to struggle and grow from it, win. Those who are not, lose!

Struggle creates winners! Michael Jordan and George Foreman are winners who are not afraid of letting people see them struggle, in order to see them win. If you want to be a success you must not be afraid of failure and learning to grow from the failures!

Thoughts are a dime a dozen . . . but the person who puts them into practice is priceless!

Until you learn to manage your money, your time and your thinking, you will never achieve anything of worth! Achievement is a choice!

The best way to build your future is to build yourself. The best way to build your company is to build your people!

All men are self made. Only the successful are willing to admit it!

Count your blessings rather than your problems and always fight for your dreams, and remember if the dream is big enough . . . the problems really don't matter!

If the dream is big enough the problems really don't matter. I couldn't stop thinking about that quote. All the way back home I thought about it and realized that it was so very true.

If the dream is big enough and you want it badly enough, the problems don't really matter, they are simply inconveniences. Will it be easy? NO! It will be hard. It will be difficult. It will be challenging, but if the dream is big enough and you want it badly enough it will happen.

How are you going to have a dream come true if you don't have a dream? To have a vision for your life, to know where you are going, is a critical step in turning a setback into a setup for a comeback. One thing that you must do when you have a setback is to ask yourself, "What is it that I want to achieve and where do I want to go?" If you know where you are going you are more apt to focus your energies on reaching that destination. Imagine you are going to work one morning and you have a flat tire when you go outside. Do you give up? NO! Because you know where you want to go and you will handle this setback in order to get to that destination.

After you get the tire straight you start out on your trip to work, but you come to a street where there is a water main break, which has created a detour. Do you give up and go back home? No! Because you know where you want to go and you take the detour and continue on toward your destination. You can see yourself reaching the destination and the setbacks are just that, a setback, a bend in the road. If you know your destination the setbacks are just detours that you go over, go around or if necessary go through, but you do not stop until you reach the destination.

The power of goals can be best illustrated by looking at an ant. Ants look toward the future expecting challenges, yet they remain focused on the goal and determined to reach it. If you look closely at an ant you will see that it is an incredible creature because it never gives up. If you see an ant going along its way and you put a leaf, a stick, or a brick or anything else in its way, it will climb over it, go under it, go around it or do whatever is necessary to get to its goal. It never stops. It will never give up. It keeps trying, keeps moving, and keeps going after its goal. In fact the only way to stop an ant and keep it from reaching its goal is to kill it. The only time an ant stops trying is when it dies.

Not only does an ant never give up, but also it is always preparing for the winter. It prepares and thinks constantly about tomorrow. The grasshopper, on the other hand, thinks only about today. The grasshopper thinks summer all summer, while the ant thinks winter all summer. When the winter comes, the ant is able to live with some comfort, while the grasshopper suffers. The lesson is that the ant works diligently to prepare for the hard times that will come because, sooner or later, they will come.

We should all take a lesson from the ant. We should work diligently every day, and we should be committed to setting goals and going after them. We should plan for tomorrow. Then we should never give up, no matter what obstacles are thrown in our way. No matter what problems beset us, or what circumstances we find ourselves in, we must never give up. We've got to keep going after our dreams and striving to reach our goals. We must always prepare for the future and think about the needs of winter while yet in the summer; we should plan and prepare for tomorrow. We should put something away for a rainy day. Just as there is sunshine, there will be rain, and just as there is summer, there is going to be winter. There will be setbacks! There will be challenges! Work hard, prepare for the difficult times and most of all . . . NEVER GIVE UP!

Ants go toward the future expecting challenges and expecting difficulties, which is why they:

1. Know what they want and know where they are going.
2. Are persistent and they never give up.
3. Set goals.
4. Plan.
5. Think about tomorrow rather than just thinking about

today (grasshoppers think summer all summer, while ants think winter all summer).

6. Work hard.

7. Work smart.

8. Choose to keep going until they get what they want or die.

The ant is a wonderful example of a creature that is totally goal oriented and does not let setbacks deter it from its goal. If we can be goal oriented and stay focused on our vision of our lives then we will start to routinely turn setbacks into setup for comebacks!

Vision is the starting point for success and it is the starting point for turning a setback into a setup for a comeback. Yet, you must keep in mind that wherever there is a vision there will be setbacks. Wherever there is a vision there will be opposition: not might be, but *will be*.

Vision and Opposition: Where You Find One You Will Always Find the Other!

Wherever you have vision you will always have opposition. You will have some challenge to the vision. You must be aware of the opposition and make preparations for it by believing it strongly and be willing to fight for it. When you have a BIG vision others will find it too much and will find it uncomfortable and will try to water it down, don't let them do it! Einstein said, "Great spirits are always faced with violent opposition from mediocre minds." You must have the vision to see, the faith to believe, the courage to do, and the strength to endure!

Reverend Willette Wright is a friend and a great preacher who shared a message in one of her sermons that hit the spot in terms of the power of a dream. She believes that in order to be successful we must take responsibility to: (1) Find our dreams, (2) Focus on your dreams, and (3) Fight for our dreams. Find it, Focus on it and Fight for it.

First, we must find the dream, because it's hard to have a dream come true if you don't have a dream. And you must realize that some of your friends will think you are crazy when you start talking about your dream and how you are going to do some incredible things in your comeback, but I implore you to dream big anyway. Every great invention, every great achievement was the result of a big dream and someone probably laughed at them, but they did it anyway.

They All Laughed

I was a guest on the Eric St. James radio show on WOL in Washington, DC, and during the conversation I mentioned that you must have a vision if you want to change your life, but you must also realize that opposition will arrive as soon as you get a vision. I said that people would call you names and life would throw all kinds of obstacles in the way, but do not despair. Every great person who has gone down in the annals of history has always had vision. They have made tough decisions, taken action and had great desire . . . and they always had opposition. Eric then mentioned a book he had read called *They All Laughed* by Ira Flatow. It is a book about people in history who did incredible things and had incredible success and how everyone laughed at them when they talked about their dreams. Every dreamer had lots of people who laughed at them, trying to discourage them.

They laughed at Thomas Edison and called him crazy when he talked about his dream of creating a bulb of light that was not a candle. They laughed at Alexander Graham Bell and called him crazy, when he talked about a machine you could talk through to other people in other places. They laughed at Christopher Columbus and called him crazy when he said the world was not flat but was round and he was willing to prove it. They laughed at the Wright brothers and called them crazy when they said they would create a flying machine.

They laughed at Martin Luther King, Jr. and called him crazy when he talked about having civil rights demonstrations that were non-violent, and when he said he wanted to have a rally on the steps of the Lincoln Memorial to share his dreams with the world, they laughed. They laughed at John F. Kennedy when he said men would reach the moon before the end of the 1960s. The list goes on and on. They all laughed!

The greatest achievements were all once considered impossible. Everyone who has done incredible things always went after the impossible. They might laugh at you and your dreams, but do not despair, you will join a very prestigious club of people who know that those who laugh last, laugh best. If you are not willing to do that which is ridiculous you cannot achieve that which is spectacular!

Next you must focus on the dream and keep it foremost in your mind. I wrote my dream in my planner and read it daily. Every time I open my planner I see my dream because I have it printed on the page divider. Remember scripture says, "Write the vision and make it plain . . . so that he who reads it may run the race!"

Finally you must be willing to fight for your dream because wherever there is a vision there will be opposition. Wherever there is a dream there will be dream-busters. And the bigger the dream the bigger the challenges and the bigger the problems, but also the bigger the rewards! It is essential that you make a commitment to fight. You must fight forward, fight back and fight on! You must realize that to turn a setback into a setup for a comeback, then you must first find your dream, then focus on your dream and then fight for your dream!

Finally we can sustain and grow the dream into a massively successful venture if we are willing to fight for the dream. You must be willing to fight for the dream, because life will test you! My mother used to tell me anything worth having is worth fighting for. The same is true for your dreams. If the dream is worth having it is worth fighting for.

The bottom line is that you must have a dream and you must make it big, because the bigger the dream the bigger the rewards. As you set out to turn a setback into a comeback, remember it will not be easy. There will be problems, there will be challenges and there will be difficulties and oppositions, but . . . if the dream is big enough, the problems don't matter! Dream Big, Fight Hard and do not worry if people laugh, because they who laugh last, laugh best!

Step 3—Teaching Points

1. If the dream is big enough, the problems don't matter. Therefore, dream big!
2. How are you going to have a dream come true if you don't have a dream?
3. Be like an ant. Keep going until you reach your goal or die, whichever comes first.
4. Plan and prepare for tomorrow. Think summer all winter and winter all summer.
5. Know wherever you find your vision you will also find opposition.
6. Winners are not afraid to let people see them struggle, in order to see them win.
7. Yes it's hard; therefore you must go at it in a hard way.
8. Be willing to fight for your dream.
9. If people are not laughing at your dreams, your dreams are not big enough.
10. Only those who are willing to try the ridiculous can achieve the spectacular.

Part II

The Power
of Decision

Step 4

···

Make Decisions: You've Had a Setback, Now What Are You Going to Do about It?

You can be the designer of your life ... or the victim of your circumstances; it's up to you!

—Redenbach

◇ ◇ ◇ In every success manual and in every interview for this book, I found the same thing over and over again. Successful people choose to be successful; they make a conscious decision. They understand that decision and choice are integral parts of the success formula. Success certainly is a choice and successful people choose to be successful! Why? Because successful people realize that setbacks are part of the price you must pay for success. In order to be successful you must deal with setbacks and learn how to overcome them or they will overcome you. They understand you may not be able to control your conditions but you can control your decisions.

You must understand the power of choice! Success is a choice! Books have stated it, speakers have spoken about it and life has shown it to be true. To be a success you must choose success, because success is not a chance, it is a choice! Rick Pitino, the coach of the Boston Celtics and the former coach of the 1996 College Champions, the Kentucky Wildcats, wrote a book called *Success is A Choice* which states that "success will not happen unless you choose to make it happen. Success is not a lucky break. It is not a divine right. It is not an accident of birth. Success is a choice!"

Stuff will happen that you cannot control but ultimately success is a matter of choice. The key to turning a setback into a comeback is first to decide. In anything in life the first thing you must do is to decide. Unfortunately most people refuse to choose and therefore choose to lose. Either you will decide for your life or life will decide for you.

When you have a setback there are a couple of critical decisions that you must make. The first decision is your perspective, how you see the setback; the second is how you will respond to the setback. These are critical decisions because they will determine how you will proceed in dealing with the setback.

React Versus Response!

> *"The circumstances that surrounds a man's life not really important. It is how the man responds to the circumstances that is important. His response is the ultimate determining factor between success and failure!"*
>
> —Booker T. Washington

Will you react to the problem, or will you respond to the challenge. It's up to you! Winners tend to respond while losers tend to react! What is the difference? Well, to react means that you see the situation from a negative perspective. Let's say you took a friend to the hospital and they were given some medicine, and then later the doctor came out and said, "Your friend had a reaction to the medication," then you would know that the medicine created a negative experience for your friend.

Yet, if you took a friend to the hospital and they were given some medicine, and then later the doctor came out and said, "Your friend responded to the medication" then you would know that the medicine created a positive experience for your friend. The same is true for your life experiences. Do you react to them or do you respond to them. Are you going to react to this setback or are you going to respond to it? It's your choice.

Decision 1: You've Had a Setback, Now What Are You Going to Do about It?

Destiny is not a chance, it is a choice! It is not a thing to be waited for, it is a thing to be achieved!
—William Jennings Bryant

The first decision when you have a setback is how are you going to view it. Is it a setback, or is it a setup for a comeback? The next decision is what are you going to do about it? Are you going to give up or are you going to keep going? Are you going to fall back or fight back? Are you going to let it stop you or let it motivate you? It is a decision that you must make. It is a choice that you, and only you can make, but the choice will have a profound impact on the results that you achieve.

Cancer? So What? It's Just a Diagnosis, Not a Death Sentence!

I was home working on this book and got a call from Les Brown, the great motivational speaker. He was in Washington and had just visited his doctor, who had treated him for prostate cancer, and he was not far from my house. I said, "Les, come on over." A short while later the doorbell rang and there he was. But he was not the Les Brown I was used to. He was slim and trim and looking great. I said, "Wow, you look great! Are you on a diet?" He said, "No! I'm on a live-it! I am no longer living to eat, I am eating to live, and having a ball."

Les told me he had become a vegetarian and was now working out every day. He was excited because his doctor had just given him a clean bill of health, and he was ecstatic. We sat down and laughed and joked as usual, but then we started talking about life. Life in terms of health, the challenges of life and the faith and choices that it takes to turn those challenges around.

I told him about the new book and how I really felt it would be wonderful to have his story, in his own words, about how he turned his cancer setback around and created a new comeback story. I said, "Les you wrote about me in your last book and I'd like to get the scoop about you, and your comeback over cancer, for my new book." Les said, "Let's do it. I want as many people as possible to hear about the fact that cancer can be beaten." He said, "I really believe God is using me to share with people that doctors give the diagnosis, but God gives the prognosis. Cancer is a diagnosis, not a death sentence. It can be beaten!"

I asked Les what he did when he was first diagnosed with cancer. Les replied, "The same things I always do when faced with challenging situations. I go through my power steps, which are: Self-Assessment, Self-Approval, Self-Commitment, and Self-Fulfillment. I used these steps years ago when I was struggling to make a living speaking and my ex-office manager embezzled thousands of dollars from me. I used these steps when I had to sleep on the floor of my office in Detroit because I had been evicted from my apartment. I used these steps when my television show was cancelled and made history as the best rated, fastest cancelled television show ever, because I refused to do topics that were low down and sleazy. I used it when I had to go through the painful loss of my mother to breast cancer. I used them when my marriage, to a woman I loved, Gladys Knight, broke up. And I used the steps to overcome prostate cancer also."

Once we started discussing his four steps I was amazed that they were very similar to my VDAD steps; we just called them by different names. *Self-Assessment* is about perspective and decision. Before you act you must realize that life is difficult and challenging, for everyone, especially those who are trying to achieve something in their lives. Then you make an assessment by first facing the fact that there is a problem, a challenge in your life, rather than running from it and sticking your head in the sand. Then assess the impact and look at it objectively. As you continue to assess the problem you must prioritize, which simply means you must make some decisions. Sometimes they will be difficult, but you must make decisions anyway.

I then asked a question that I knew the answer to, but wanted to hear it anyway. "Les, why does it happen to you? What do you say about the fact that you have had all of these challenges?" Then he responded, as I knew he would. "It's like the story about the lady who had an accident and asked why did it have to happen to her? The ambulance driver asked her, who do you suggest, Oprah? It happens to everyone, everyone gets a turn." This confirmed my theory of Recognition: setbacks are a part of life, they happen to everyone.

Next we discussed *Self-Approval*, which is about vision. It is about how you must see yourself and how you then determine what you need to do to overcome this challenge. First, you must feel good about yourself and know that you are capable of overcoming this issue. Second, you must focus your energies on your goal and on what you must do to achieve the goal and to remain positive in the face of the challenge. Les said that he was afraid when he got the diagnosis but realized that he had to focus on his faith rather than his fears, to overcome the problem.

Next was *Self-Commitment*, which is about action. It is about having the discipline and commitment to keep trying, no matter what. He made some decisions that were uncomfortable, yet necessary to turn the setback into a comeback. He knew he had to lose weight, so he changed his lifestyle and made a commitment to becoming a vegetarian. He also made a commitment to exercise daily (the only other exercise he used to do was lift the pack of M&Ms up to his mouth). He decided to work out every day, even when traveling.

Finally, he used *Self-Fulfillment*, which is consistent with my power principle called Desire. It is to focus on how badly you want it, and a dual focus on faith, and a knowledge that God is good, all the time. Even when you have challenges, trust God and have faith that He will never leave you nor forsake you. To realize that to overcome your challenges you must understand the power of prayer and that you must work on the complete person, physically, mentally and spiritually. It takes all three parts to effectively overcome the challenges of life and find personal fulfillment. Faith, hope and love of self and others leads to fulfillment. And then you add desire, which leads to fulfillment, which leads to empowerment; and empowerment leads to turning your obstacles into opportunities.

Les Brown shares a message of overcoming because of what he has overcome. From being born in an abandoned building and being adopted with his twin brother, when he was six days old. From being labeled educabley mentally retarded, flunking two grades, barely graduating high school, and never going to college to becoming one of the most quoted and highest paid public speakers in the world. From starting his working career as a sanitation worker to becoming a popular radio disc jockey, community activist and then state legislator.

From cancer victim to cancer victor, Les Brown is an over-comer, who knows how to turn setbacks into setups for comebacks. As Les said in his last book, *It's Not Over Until You Win.*

It truly is not over until you win! You must remember that! Never give up, keep trying and you can turn it around! In fact you must keep in mind that as long as you're breathing you still have a chance, a shot, an opportunity to turn it all around! Keep living, keep trying, and never give up and you can turn a setback into a setup for a comeback!

I Decided to Believe Mama

Another great story of never giving up and staying committed to your goal, is the story of Wilma Rudolph, the great track star and Olympic Medal winner. Here is a brief recap of her story and how she used vision and decision to turn her challenges into champion moments.

Wilma Rudolph was born in Clarksville Tennessee, the seventeenth of nineteen children. Her mother was a maid and her father was a store clerk. They didn't have a lot of money but they did have a lot of love. At the age of four, little Wilma was stricken with polio and was crippled in one leg. Her parents took her to the hospital, which was about a hundred miles away, and the doctors told her that she would not walk again.

Wilma was heartbroken because she loved to run and play with her brothers and sisters. On the long ride home she kept thinking about what the doctors had said and started to cry. Her parents sat with her and talked to her and told her, "Baby, I know the doctors said that you were not going to be able to run again, but I don't believe they were right. I believe God is going to heal you and that you will run again, and will run fast." Little Wilma made a decision right then and there. She said, "I had heard what the doctors said and I had heard what Mama said, and I've decided to believe Mama!"

She started working on herself, little by little. First she worked on standing, then walking, then walking fast, then jogging and then running. It was difficult, it was uncomfortable, but fifteen years later Wilma Rudolph became the first American woman to win three goal medals in the Olympics. She believed that she could run, she decided to do whatever was necessary to make her dream a reality and she worked on herself daily so she could learn to run and then she took action and she did run . . . and she ran fast!

Decision and belief are keys to turning your setbacks into comebacks. You must decide and then believe in the decision. Like the man who was given six months to live but he decided to live twenty-five years more. He believed he could, he believed he would, and he did! Decision and belief are powerful ingredients in turning your setbacks into comebacks.

Every day I pray for wisdom and courage because I found that these two ingredients are necessary for success, personally as well as professionally. Wisdom is the ability to discern and make good decisions. Then you need courage to act on those decisions. It takes courage to take a stand on your dreams and courage to move forward to make them a reality. Wisdom to make wise decisions, and courage to act on them are my constant prayer in the process of turning my setbacks into comeback. I recommend that you pray for wisdom and courage.

Step 4—Teaching Points

1. Remember success is a choice, not a chance. Choose to be successful.
2. Decide for life, or life will decide for you.

3. It is not the circumstances that are important, it is how you respond to the circumstances.
4. Choose to respond not react.
5. Doctors give the diagnosis, God gives the prognosis.
6. If they give you six months to live, decide to live twenty more years.
7. Remember, it's not over until you win!
8. As long as you're breathing, you've still got a chance to comeback.
9. Decide to work on yourself.
10. Pray for wisdom and courage, every day.

Step 5

Do Not Panic! There's No Power in a Panic! Decide to Stay Calm, Stay Collected and Stay Positive!

> *The only "good luck" most great people ever had was being born with the ability and determination to overcome "bad luck!"*
>
> —Channing Pollock

◇ ◇ ◇ When you have a challenge in your life you might not know what to do, but one thing you definitely should not do is to panic. You should not panic, because there is no power in a panic! Panic is taken from the Greek word "to choke". To choke means to cut off, to disengage, and to disconnect. When you panic that is exactly what you do. You cut off the air to your brain, and if you cut off air to the brain then you cannot think clearly, and if you cannot think clearly you cannot exercise all of your options and if you cannot exercise your options you cannot make good decisions. And it is clear that you must make wise decisions if you want to turn your setbacks into comebacks. That is why you must not panic, because panic short-circuits the nervous system and keeps you from thinking rational thoughts. In fact, panic really makes you crazy.

History has shown multiple examples of people who panicked, and lost everything. During the stock market crash of 1929, thousands of people panicked and committed suicide, not knowing that life does go on, and if you built it once, you can build it again. Do not panic, especially with extreme measures like suicide. Suicide is a permanent solution for a temporary problem, and is usually the result of panic.

In the Broadway play *Annie* there is a wonderful song titled "Tomorrow" that speaks to the fact that no matter what problems you might have today, no matter what challenges you might have today, have hope and remember that the sun "will" come out tomorrow. Have faith and know that tomorrow brings a brand new day, a brand new opportunity to turn those problems around and to turn those setbacks into comebacks. You will have setbacks but as scripture says "it came to pass" . . . therefore it did not come to stay. You might have some Friday situations, some major setbacks, but always remember that Sunday, the sure victory, is on the way. Just don't panic, 'cause Sunday is a-coming, and the sun will come out tomorrow—just keep going!

Maintain a Positive Attitude!

Gravity is a fact, but airplanes circumvent that fact on an hourly basis.

—Neil Armstrong

Your attitude is more important than the facts!

—Ken Meninger

The fact is that Mugsy Bouges was born short of stature, but his attitude was he wanted to play professional basketball, and he did it. Roger Crawford, the great speaker, author and semi-pro tennis player, was born without hands and with only one leg, but his attitude is "that is only an inconvenience." He says that he cannot eat with chopsticks or play chopsticks on the piano, but he has gone on to become a national tennis champion, as well as a world-renowned speaker and author of the national bestseller, *How High Can You Bounce?* He understands that it is your attitude, not your aptitude that ultimately determines your altitude.

Attitude is a choice. It is a decision. Decide to have a positive attitude! As Dennis Brown says, "The only difference between a good day and a bad day is your attitude." You must choose it. We can all have short-term happiness, even if we have a bad attitude. We might buy a car or get a job or meet someone who is Mr. or Ms. "Right" and we will be happy . . . for the moment. In order to maintain that happiness and sustain that happiness, you must develop a positive attitude, because the car will get older and will eventually need servicing, the job could change and change fast, and Mr. or Ms. "Right" could become Mr. or Ms. "Wrong!" In order to overcome the challenges and problems of life it is essential that you have a positive attitude, mentally and emotionally. You need a positive mental attitude so you can think in a positive manner and a positive emotional attitude so you can act in a positive way.

With a positive attitude you can find some good in the bad, and some happiness in the sad. With a positive attitude you expect good things to come your way and you therefore attract good things your way. With a positive attitude you tend to be more enthusiastic about life and therefore life will be more enthusiastic about you. With a positive attitude you simply handle problems better!

It's all about attitude. You must have a positive attitude. And how do you get a positive attitude? You decide to. It is a decision. It is a choice. You cannot control what happens to you. You cannot control what happens around you, but you can control what happens in you. Choose to have a positive attitude.

Keep my words positive, because my words become behaviors.

Keep my behaviors positive, because my behaviors become habits.

Keep my habits positive, because my habits become my values.

Keep my values positive, because they become my destiny.

—Mohatma Gandhi

Your Input Determines Your Output!

"You are what you eat." That is what all the diet books say about your health. And computer people talk about GIGO, which means, "garbage in, garbage out!" The same is true for life; you are what you put in. Bestselling author, Dennis Waitley, talks about the fact that if you take an orange and squeeze it, what will come out? Orange juice! If you squeeze a grape what will come out? Grape juice! Why? Because when pressure is applied the true internal essence will come out. What ever you put into your mind is essentially what you will become, that is why you must make a commitment to putting in positive information, on a daily basis. Life will throw challenges at us on a daily basis and can apply extreme pressure and that is when what you put in will get overwhelming, especially if you don't have a base from which to offset the challenges. It is critical that you use great care in what goes in our mind and in your spirit. You must be careful that you do not allow your mind and spirit to be infected by negative influences. It all adds up to attitude. Decide to have a positive attitude.

Attitude Is Everything! Don't Tighten up . . . Lighten up!

Keith Harrell is a friend who co-authored a book with me called *Only the Best on Success!* Keith has a great story about overcoming setbacks and turning them into comebacks. Keith worked for IBM for fourteen years and expected to be there until he retired. Yet one Friday afternoon Keith and 650 of his co-workers were asked to come to a special meeting. At the meeting they were told that IBM was announcing their first layoff in their sixty-five-year history. They were told that 80 percent of those employees would be gone in three months.

Keith shared with me that at that moment fear was in the room, uncertainty was in the room, anxiety was gripping the crowd, some were shaking and getting physically ill. After the announcement was made Keith jumped up and said, "I have a question!" He was asked, "What is your question, young man?" Keith replied, "Well, sir, once the 80 percent are gone . . . Can I get a bigger office, one with a window view?" The room broke up in laughter. Keith said he realized that humor was necessary at that moment to help people to get a grip and to help people keep from falling apart. A good friend nudged him and said, "Hey Keith . . . Mr. Positive, you know you'll probably be the first to go!" And, HE WAS!!!!! He was fired from a job that he thought he would never be fired from, a job he was planning to retire from. He had a major setback!

Keith didn't fall apart. He had been reading the positive books and listening to the motivational tapes and he had a positive attitude. Keith took that positive attitude and mixed that with a positive aptitude. He started working on his dream of being a speaker and trainer and decided to share with others how to handle change with a positive attitude. He went on to build a multimillion-dollar motivational speaking and training company. He is the author of the bestselling book, *Attitude Is Everything* and is well known in board rooms across the country as "Mr. Superfantastic" because of his greeting to all of his audiences, where he says, "When people ask you how you are doing, just say . . . Superfantastic!"

One of the most important things dealing with your attitude is the people you associate with. You must make a clear decision to stop hanging around with negative, small-minded people because they will poison your possibility thinking and therefore hinder your turning your setback into a setup for a comeback.

People with Possibility Blindness

One of the keys to overcoming setbacks is to stay away from negative people who will try to talk you out of getting up and living your dreams. You must also align with positive people who will encourage you. Many times when you have a setback you will have friends and family members who will try to talk you out of trying again. They will say, "Don't try to do that! You know you just had a setback and it will be painful if you don't make it!" Or they will say, "Aunt Susie tried to do that and she didn't make it. Don't try, it will be painful if you don't make it!" Friends, I have found that the majority of people who try to talk you out of going after your dream are not trying to be mean spirited. They just happen to suffer from possibility blindness. Since it didn't happen for them or for someone else, then they think it cannot happen for you! WRONG! That is not true! Nothing is more rewarding than to watch someone who says it can't be done get interrupted by someone who is actually doing it.

To tell people you love to stop trying when they fall down is the same as telling the baby, "Don't try to walk anymore. You fell down so just stay down. It will be painful!" Of course it will be painful but without falling down the baby will never learn to walk. If you are not willing to fail, it is really difficult to be able to succeed.

Michael Jordan, who is said to be the greatest basketball player of all times, spoke on a television commercial about his failures and how they were the reason for his success . . . He said, "I have missed more than nine thousand shots in my career. I have lost almost three hundred games. On twenty-six occasions I have been entrusted to take the game winning shot . . . and missed. And I have failed over and over and over again in my life. And that is why . . . I succeed." It is because of his willingness to fail, his willing to take risks, that he is able to succeed.

Decide to be more excited about winning than afraid of losing. It's a choice. Decide to get and keep a positive attitude; it is a choice. Remember that people with a positive attitude attract more good to themselves than people with negative attitudes. So choose not to worry, choose to be positive and choose to stay calm and collected and connected. As Bobby McFerrin sang, "Don't Worry, Be Happy!" How? Choose to, it is a choice!

WHY WORRY?
Submitted by Janice Krouskop

There are only two things to worry about;
Either you are well or you are sick.
If you are well, there is nothing to worry about.
If you are sick, there are two things to worry about;
Either you will get well or you will die.
If you get well, there is nothing to worry about.
If you die, there are only two things to worry about;
Either you will go to Heaven or you will go to Hell.
If you go to Heaven, there is nothing to worry about.
If you go to Hell, well . . . why worry now! It's Too Late!

Author Unknown

Step 5—Teaching Points

1. Do not panic. There's no power in a panic.
2. Practice and talk yourself into being calm.

3. Do not awfullize and catastrophize; stop adding loss to loss.

4. When you have "Friday" situations, remember that "Sunday" is on the way.

5. No matter how bad things are today, tomorrow is on the way. Hold On!

6. Remember your attitude is more important than the facts.

7. Decide to win with whatever hand you're given.

8. Don't tighten up, lighten up.

9. Nothing is more rewarding than to watch those who say it can't be done get interrupted by those actually doing it.

10. Take a chance and be willing to fail, because only then can you truly succeed.

Part III

The Power
of Action

◇ ◇ ◇ In the last chapter we talked about the power of asking and how the scripture of "asking, seeking and knocking" teaches us about the power of asking, but there is also another teaching point that can be extracted from that scripture, which is the importance of action. Ask and you shall receive, seek and ye shall find, knock and the door will be opened unto you. For everyone that asks, receives, and everyone that seeks, finds, and everyone that knocks the door is opened unto them. Notice that each one of these points is connected to an action statement. If you take the action, then you will get the blessing. Most people receive not because they ask not, seek not and knock not! Those who act are those who get. You must take action if you want to get results.

Step 6

· ·

Take Action: You Can Have Lights, You Can Have Cameras, but Nothing Happens until You Take Action!

> *On the sands of hesitation, lay the bones of countless millions*
> *Who at the dawn of victory, sat down and waited, and in waiting died.*
>
> —Evangeline Wilkes

> *Sometimes you must fake it until you make it . . . Act yourself into a new way of thinking and think yourself into a new way of acting.*
>
> —Willie Jolley

◇ ◇ ◇ The next thing you need to turn a setback into a setup for a comeback is action. A vision without action is an illusion, and action without a vision is confusion. But action and vision, desire and decision can change your life and can change the world. Or as Marlon Smith, the great motivational trainer says, "A vision without action is a wish, and wishes have no substance."

Earlier we talked about the fact that ants have an innate understanding of the importance of having a goal and the hard work and persistence necessary to make that goal a reality. Ants understand that hard work is a critical element in the quest to reach your goals. Hard work is the key. This is an excerpt from my book, *It Only Takes A Minute To Change Your Life* that speaks about hard work.

Hard Work Works

I received a call from my friend Amy Goldson, with a quote that she got from her mother that was very helpful in her quest to become a lawyer. The quote simply stated, "Hard work, works!" And that is true! There is no substitute for hard work. Success is not the result of luck or good fortune, but rather of hard work and persistence. In Proverbs it states that, "Hard work brings prosperity, while playing around brings poverty!" It might be uncomfortable but it is absolutely necessary to work hard and persist, if you are serious about turning your setbacks into comebacks. The only place where success comes before work is in the dictionary.

William Penn wrote, "No pain, no palm; No cross, no crown; No thorn, no throne; No gall, no glory!" Janice Krouskop says it so well when she said, "Without ambition one starts nothing, and without hard work one finishes nothing. Therefore those who stretch their backbone to reach their wishbone will make things happen!" I believe that says it all, first there is the goal of what you want to achieve, then comes hard work followed by determination and persistence.

Persistence and perseverance are essential elements in the quest to turn a setback into a setup for a comeback. It might seem like this ingredient almost seems to go without saying, but let me tell you it needs to be said over and over again. It needs to be said in the morning at noon and then again at night, in fact it needs to be said during your dreams! Persist . . . Never give up!

W. Mitchell exemplifies the power of decision and the power of choosing success. W. Mitchell is a friend who constantly inspires me. I first heard about W. Mitchell via a Zig Ziglar tape. Then I heard Anthony Robbins talk about him and then many others after that. I first met him at The National Speakers Association and we became friends, in fact he wrote the introduction for my last book. Mitchell is an inspiration because of his willingness to turn setbacks into comebacks over and over again. His story is legendary because he is a person who exemplifies turning setbacks into comebacks.

The Man Who Would Not Be Defeated, W. Mitchell

W. Mitchell is a man who exemplifies turning setbacks into setups for comebacks. He is respectfully called "the man who would not be defeated" because he never gives up. Twenty-five years ago Mitchell was a student who worked part-time as a cable operator in San Francisco. Between school and work, he found time to ride his new Harley Davidson motorcycle for recreation. He lived for times when he could get out on his bike and feel the refreshing wind blow on his face.

One day while taking a ride, Mitchell was crossing an intersection and suddenly saw a truck running a red light. The truck slammed into him and he was slammed to the ground, and as he lay there in agony he smelled gas and realized that he was covered with it. Suddenly there was an explosion and the bike went up in flames, and then the fire spread and soon engulfed Mitchell in flames. He became a human torch and was completely burned from head to toe. He lost his fingers and toes and was left with no resemblance to his former self. He went through months and months of agonizing surgery and rehabilitation. He had a setback but he made a decision, he would not give up!

He finished his education and went on to start a business that soon became very successful. In fact, he was able to purchase a private plane that he piloted. His plane became his passion and he spent all of his spare time flying. One evening, while in flight, the plane started experiencing engine problems. He attempted to land but lost control and crashed. When he awoke after months in a coma, he found that now he was paralyzed from the waist down! He sat and looked at himself and saw a burned man who was now paralyzed and forced to live the rest of his life in a wheelchair. He had a setback, but he decided not to give up!

Mitchell started saying, "You cannot control what happens to you but you can control what you do about it." He continued to fight for his dream and continued to make a difference. He has gone on to become one of the top motivational speakers in the world. He owns homes in Colorado, California and Hawaii. He truly lives life to the fullest. He lives the life that he talks about. It's not what happens to you that counts. It's what you do about it.

You cannot give up; you have to fight on. You must make up your mind that giving up is just not an option. It must be a part of your make up, something that you have pre-programmed way deep inside . . . giving up is not an option. I heard a person once say that "Nothing is stronger than a made up mind" and I must agree. When you absolutely, positively make up your mind, you have created a powerful force. Resolve to become unstoppable.

Unfortunately most people never really make up their minds. They think they might like to do something but have not truly made up their minds and therefore are easily swayed by the challenges and circumstances. Am I saying that if you make up your mind you are guaranteed to win in everything you do? NO! There are no guarantees in life, but I can say that if you give up you are guaranteed NOT to win! If you want to overcome a setback and turn it into a comeback you must make a predetermined decision that you will not give up! You just can't give up!

In order to overcome the challenging times and situations that life throws at you it is essential that you make a predetermined decision to never give up. Those people who have turned their setbacks around always had a commitment to keep going, they decided that giving up was simply not an option. They went into the fight with confidence, determination and persistence. Confidence came as a result of their belief in themselves. It was tied into their faith. They realized that faith is an essential part of every success story.

Mandela! Mandela!

When individuals rise above their circumstances and use problems to push them to become more, they grasp greatness.

—Nelson Mandela

Nelson Mandela is a legend in his own time and one of the best stories of someone who understood that a setback is nothing but a setup for a comeback. He was a young lawyer who was jailed because he refused to accept the apartheid system in South Africa. He was in jail for twenty-seven years and was consistently offered his freedom if he would make a public statement that he was accepting of apartheid, but he refused. The South African government offered him money and privileges, but he refused. Mandela was finally released after twenty-seven years, but that was not the end of this incredible comeback. First he helped to orchestrate the end of apartheid in South Africa, and a few years later he became the first black president of South Africa. From prisoner to president! Oh, what a way to turn a setback into a setup for a comeback!

Know What Is NO!

Sometimes you will have setbacks when people slam doors in your face and tell you "NO!" Well, I say that a "NO" is nothing but a "Yes," waiting to a happen. Sometimes people will just say no to you because they aren't sure how serious you are. Sometimes people will say "No" because that it is the easiest thing to say. People will say "No" and think that will get you to give up, which is does for most people. The achiever though doesn't let a "No" break their spirit. They understand that a "No" doesn't mean you should give up, it sometimes means you must try again in a different way. They understand that persistence is the key to changing a "No" into a "Yes," because persistence always breaks down resistance! What is a "No?" It is nothing but a "Yes" waiting to happen. Is it a setback? NOOOO! It is just a setup for a comeback!

Determination is the next step. Many people get the words determination and persistence confused. They feel they are the same, but they are quite different. Persistence is an action, determination is an attitude. Determination is the attitude that allows you to keep going in spite of the problems, in spite of the challenges. I have a quote above my desk, which states, "The bulldog is one of nature's most determined creatures and the nose of the bulldog is slanted backwards so he can continue to breathe without letting go!" We must be like the bulldog and simply never give up. Become confident, determined and persistent and learn to breathe without letting go!

I like to share with audiences that the key to success in any venture is just to keep going, keep trying. The old saying states that "winners never quit and quitters never win," and there is truth in that statement. The real fact is that many times the only difference in a winner and a loser is that the winner just kept trying. They may not have had any more talent or any more ability, but they just kept going. When the going got tough, they just kept going. Zig Ziglar has a saying, "The difference between a big shot and a little shot is a big shot is a little shot who just kept on shooting!" I truly believe that the key to success in any venture is to make a commitment to keep going, in fact it is critical. When you have the vision you will also have opposition and that is when you must persist and never give up!

> *Step back, take a deep breath, cry if necessary . . . but then get back up and get back at it*
>
> —Willie Jolley

Folks, we all get tired, and need to step back sometimes, but the winners get back into the fight quickly and keep fighting until they get what they want. Then they get ready for the next battle, because they understand that life is challenging and setbacks are a part of the challenge. It is a part of life! Know that tomorrow is a brand-new day, and has brand-new opportunities. Along with the new day they realize that there will be new challenges, but they have developed the will to face each challenge as it comes. Scripture says do not worry about tomorrow's problems, let tomorrow handle the problems of tomorrow. Focus on today and enjoy the ride. As my friend Larry Winget says "Expect the best, prepare for the worst and celebrate it all!"

I Quit!

My son and I were riding by the place where I used to work. My son was about six years old at the time and he asked, "Dad, isn't that where you used to work?" I said, "Yes it is." He then asked, "Dad did you get fired or laid off?" I replied, "No son, I Quit!" As I said that the tears welled up in his eyes and he said, "Daddy, you quit? You quit? But, Daddy, you told me never give up, you said I should never ever give up. And you quit?" And as the tears rolled down his cheeks I pulled the car over to the curb, wiped away his tears and said, "William, I'm going to give you a life lesson, son. See, Yes I quit! But not because I was giving up! I quit, because I was going up!" Friends, sometimes you have to quit those things that keep you down, you have to quit those things that make you frown, you have to quit those things that keep you bound. As Rosita Perez says, "You must be willing to jump . . . and grow wings on the way down!" What is it in your life that you need to "quit" in order to go up? Sometimes you must change directions and strategies in order to reach your dream, but you must never stop trying. Remember, the magic of triumph is the first syllable . . . try.

Step 6—Teaching Points

1. Take action because a vision without action is a wish and wishes have no substance.
2. Hard work works.
3. Without ambition nothing gets started and without hard work nothing gets finished.
4. It's not what happens to you that counts, it's what you do about it.
5. A "No" is nothing but a "Yes" waiting to happen.
6. Persistence breaks down resistance.
7. Be like the bulldog; learn to breathe without letting go.
8. Expect the best, prepare for the worst and celebrate it all.
9. Nothing is stronger than a made-up mind, therefore make up your mind.
10. Quit those things that keep you down, keep you bound and make you frown.

Step 7

··

Take Responsibility:
Face It, Trace It, Erase It Replace It!

*You may not be responsible for being knocked down
but you are responsible for getting back up!*

◇ ◇ ◇ The next step in the process of turning a setback into a comeback, is to take responsibility, which is to face it, trace it, erase it and replace it. It doesn't matter whether you caused the setback, or whether it was thrust upon you, you must take responsibility if you want to turn it into a comeback! Why? Because it is *your life, and you must take responsibility for your life!*

I know some setbacks are so painful and so unfair that you want to run and hide. But you must understand that ultimately the setback is your responsibility because our response to the setbacks ultimately determines our direction in life. We may not be able to control or choose the circumstances but we can choose the response. Case in point is Mrs. Doris DeBoe, whom I wrote about in earlier books, who is a four-time cancer survivor. She cannot control the fact that cancer continues to appear in her life but she decided to win in spite of the cancer. Her favorite saying is "I might have cancer but cancer does not have me!" She has made a conscious decision to take responsibility for her challenges, no matter how they appear, and she has decided to win and has beat cancer four times. We must take the hand we are dealt and learn to win with it.

Some setbacks are things that happen to us that we cannot control, but other setbacks are often the results of our choices. We participate in the creation of some of our setbacks. In other words, we "mess up" and create "self-made" setbacks. We all sometimes have lapses in judgment, make mistakes, make poor choices and create our own setbacks. I don't know about you but I have done some things that were just plain stupid and have created some of my own setbacks. It was not my intention to create a problem, but the end result was I created a self-made setback, and it was my responsibility to fix it.

When we have a setback due to our errors in judgment, we must be willing to accept the fact that we are part of the problem, and therefore must be part of the solution. We must take responsibility, face it, say "I messed up," and go about fixing it. One of the best examples of someone who made a mistake and then took responsibility and turned it into a comeback is Vanessa Williams. She understood that you truly can turn a setback into a comeback, if you are willing to face it, trace it, erase it and replace it and take responsibility.

Vanessa Williams made history in 1984 when she became the first African American to win the Miss America crown, but less than a year later the crown was taken away because it was discovered that she had had explicit photographs taken during her college years. It was a mistake. An example of poor judgment that came back to haunt her. It was a devastating setback. She lost her crown and her "girl next door" image.

She was disappointed, embarrassed, humiliated, but she was not a quitter. She disappeared for a short while and many thought that would be the end of Vanessa Williams, but they were wrong. She came back stronger than ever. She showed us that a setback really is nothing but a setup for a comeback.

What were the things she did in turning her setback into a

comeback? The first thing she did was to pray, because she said, "When you pray, you find the answer." Second she made the decision to hold fast to her dreams and never give up. Third she realized that she still had talent and she worked hard to showcase her singing and acting talents. She started recording beautiful love songs and became a bestselling recording artist, eventually winning an Academy Award for her rendition for the theme song for the movie, *Pocahontas*. She then moved to television and the stage, even winning rave reviews for a starring role on Broadway in the hit play *Kiss Of The Spider Woman*.

She went on to do movies. She started with small parts, but they soon realized she was a bona fide actress and she went on to become a box office superstar. She even starred with Arnold Schwarzenegger, who told her, "You are not just a survivor, you are a thriver. You showed the world that you are not just a pretty face, but you have guts, courage and perseverance. You came back and proved you are truly a winner!"

Vanessa Williams showed us that we all make mistakes, and our mistakes create some of our setbacks. But even those setbacks can be overcome, if you are willing to take responsibility.

Webster's defines "responsibility" as being morally, legally and mentally accountable. I say that responsibility also means that you must respond with ability, all of your ability.

In fact, to respond with all of your natural-born abilities. I mentioned Keith Harrell earlier in the book regarding his Superfantastic Attitude! He told me of a story where he was getting off a plane, on his way to a speech, and someone asked him "Do you play with the NBA?" (Keith is 6 foot 7 inches tall and was a college basketball player). Keith stopped, looked the person in the eye, and said, "Yes! I do play with the NBA . . . I play with my natural born ability, and I am slam dunking every day!" You too must respond to life with your natural born ability. You must play the game of life with all that you have, as hard as you can and take responsibility for your success or your failure.

Steps for Responding with Ability

To take responsibility, and respond with your natural born abilities, you need to employ four steps, which are:

1. Face It!

> *Face your problems and acknowledge them, but do not*
> *let them master you!*
>
> —Helen Keller

The first thing I do when I have a setback, a problem, a difficulty in my life is to face it and realize that there is a problem. Acknowledgment is the first step to resolution. If you act like an ostrich and stick your head in the sand, you might miss a few problems but you will also miss a great number of opportunities.

You cannot solve the problem if you don't acknowledge the problem. It's like the lady who didn't want to face the fact that her bills were more than her income, so she just started putting the bills in a dresser drawer and ignoring them. She figured they would go away. WRONG! You must be willing to face up to your setback if you want to turn it into a comeback.

The first step to recovery from anything is to first admit that there is a problem. Whether it is a drug problem, an alcohol problem, a sex problem, or whether you lost a job, or lost a loved one. You must face it so you can then look at the options, make appropriate decisions, take appropriate action and move on. Remember, wherever there are challenges there are always opportunities.

After I acknowledge there is a problem the next thing I do is pray. I told you earlier, when I have a setback I always take a minute to pray for wisdom and courage. I pray for wisdom so I can know what to do, and courage so I will be strong enough to do what is necessary. And I do not always pray for God to fix it, but rather for God to help me face it, because I know if I can face it, then He can help me fix it! After I pray, then I know it is time to act, because prayer and action go hand and hand. First pray then PUSH, which means to Push Until Something Happens. You must take action. Scripture says, "Faith without works is dead." Faith must be manifested in action. Therefore you should pray like it all depends on God, and work like it all depends on you!

Discover Your Strength!

Cindy Jones is another great example of facing a setback and moving on to turn it into a comeback. In 1962, when Cindy Jones was a 26-year-old housewife, her husband went to work one morning and never returned. The phone call from the hospital said he had been killed in an automobile accident. She was devastated. Her heart was broken, her dreams shattered. There was an overwhelming silence in her life.

Four days later, she went to the hospital and gave birth to her second son. She felt like she was living her life "out of sequence." Babies are supposed to be born long before fathers die. Mothers of babies are supposed to have daddies to help them. In just a short time, the shape of her family had changed from two parents and one child to one parent and two children.

Fear consumed her! Fear of going on, fear of the relentless pain for which there was no relief. Nothing seemed safe or dependable anymore. But she realized she had to face it; she couldn't just cop out! As the sole supporter of two children, she needed a career and a regular paying job. She had to face it, and she did.

She made up her mind that she would take an active role in the rebuilding of her life rather than let things happen by chance. She wanted to make certain her life represented the best that was within her. That forced her to look deep inside, to find her own uniqueness, her own special attributes and abilities, inner strengths and talents.

A few months after her husband's death, she took the money they had been saving for a new home and went back to school for a teacher's certificate. As a grieving widow, and mother of two, she started classes on a cold January day at the University of Michigan. As she walked into class the first day was extremely painful and lonely. She really struggled to push through her pain. She prayed for strength to continue to face it.

She went on to become a successful teacher, then a national speaker, and president of her own consulting firm. She faced her problems and was able to rise above her circumstances and overcome the challenges, even though they were initially bleak and life shattering. She found that the pull of the future was much more powerful than the push of the past. Finally she said she learned that life is much like a 10-speed bicycle—often we have gears we never use until we are forced to. We can all start using all our gears from wherever we are, with whatever challenges we have, but first we must fact them.

2. Trace It!
Where did the problem originate and what can you learn from the experience? To trace it you must look back and see what you can learn from the setback and also see if you had anything to do with creating the problem. Was there something you could have done differently? If so, you can learn from this and not make the same mistake twice (once is a mistake, twice is stupid). Sometimes it occurs in relationships. Many people have

setbacks in relationships and then go back and do the exact same thing in the next relationship. Others get hurt, and take the opposite extreme. They give up on love and relationships totally.

We should learn by our past experiences, not give up on relationships. It just means that you use better judgment and more wisdom in future decisions. There is an old story about a little boy who smelled hot rolls in the kitchen and went to get one and touched the pan, which was still hot. He burned his hand and didn't touch any more pans, hot or cold, and gave up eating rolls because he was afraid he would burn his hands.

Wisdom would suggest that the next time he smelled the rolls and wanted a hot roll he would test it before touching it, or get a pot holder or oven mitt, so as not to burn his hand, not give up on rolls. We must learn from our past experiences, yet we must not throw the baby out with the bath water. Don't give up on people or relationships because you once got burned by other people and in other relationships. Don't stop enjoying life because you have a few bumps along the way. Life is for living, not for shrinking away from! And the greatest mistake a person can make is to be so afraid of making a mistake that they do nothing! It's okay to make a mistake; just learn from it!

A reporter asked a bank president:

"Sir, what is the secret of your success?"

"Two words."

"And, sir, what are they?"

"Right decisions."

"And how do you make the right decisions?"

"One word."

"And, sir, what is it?"

"Experience."

"And how do you get experience?"

"Usually . . . it's because of wrong decisions, if you learn from them. That creates experience."

Successful people learn from past mistakes and make adjustments for the future. If you don't do that you can create a cycle of mistakes, which leads to you beating yourself up. This leads to lower self-esteem, which leads to negative feelings about yourself and your decisions, which leads to more bad decisions. Then you start the cycle over again with more negative self-talk and lower esteem and more bad decision. STOP THE MADNESS! If you make a mistake, so be it! Learn from it and keep going.

3. Erase It!

You have traced the problem and faced the problem, then you must erase the problem. Do not dwell on it, and do not beat yourself up. Learn from the mistake, make a commitment to do better in the future and let it go! We all make mistakes, that is why they put erasers on pencils and delete keys on computers. The old saying states, "Experience is the best teacher . . . but experience is usually the result of mistakes!" Forgive yourself and move on.

There are two types of mistakes: those that teach and those that destroy. We can either see those mistakes as learning experiences or we can see them as death shots. We can see them either as our teacher or our undertaker. It is our choice! I recommend that you make it your teacher. Let them stretch you and help you to expand and broaden your horizon. Mistakes are a part of life and they can be a great teaching tool; but remember, the biggest mistake is to try not to make any mistakes, because then you are doomed to fail! As Edison said, "I didn't fail ten thousand times in making the light bulb; I found ten thousand new ways that didn't work!" And Albert Einstein said, "It's not a failure, if you learn from it!"

No one great became great without making mistakes.

Mistakes are a part of growth and a necessary part of success. You cannot change what has happened in the past, but you can fix some of the things you have done in the past. One way to erase the problem is to go back and fix things that have been bothering you so you can move on. If you have hurt someone in the past and the memory still bothers you, go back and apologize. If you borrowed from someone, then repay them. Fix the mistakes as best as you can, learn from your experiences and move on. If you need to step back and fix something, do it. You do not have to dwell there, fix it and move forward!

4. Replace It!
Once you have faced it, traced it, and erased it, then you must replace it. And there will be people, places and things in your life that just beg to be replaced. Do them a favor and grant their wish; leave them alone and replace them. Replace the negative element with a positive element and move to a place of peace, purpose and passion. Make a decision, choose to be positive and focus on the positive rather than the negative.

Change your self-communication. Do not beat yourself up. Make a commitment to change your self-talk. No more negative communication. Your self-talk impacts your self-image and your self-image impacts your behavior, which then impacts your self-talk and the cycle continues on and on.

Sweet Talk Yourself

To change your life you must change your communication and make it a point to have positive self-talk. Sweet talk yourself and speak positive into your life, speak good into your life; there is power in words. Sticks and stones may break your bones . . . but words can break your spirit. Watch what you allow you to say to you, and to others. First, speak "good" to yourself! Always speak "good" to and of yourself! Love yourself and be willing to tell yourself that you love you.

I tell students to be careful of conceit, yet they should love themselves. I remember when I was young, one girl would say to another, "You think you're cute" and they would deny that they thought they were cute. As I got older I thought about it and realized how stupid it is to deny that you can be cute. You ought to think you are cute; it is much nicer than thinking you are ugly. Do not accept anyone's opinion that belittles you. If God made you then you are beautiful. Period!

In order to turn a setback into a setup for a comeback you must take responsibility and respond with your natural born ability. You must see that with every burden there is a blessing, and with every blessing there is a burden. A burden of responsibility, to trace it, face it, erase it and replace it. Try it, you'll not just go through it, but you will also grow through it.

Step 8—Teaching Points

1. You may not be responsible for getting knocked down, but you are responsible for getting back up.
2. Respond with your abilities, your NBA (natural born abilities).
3. Face it: acknowledge the problem and pray not just to fix it, but to help you face it.
4. Trace it: Look at the problem and see if you had anything to do with the creation of the problem.
5. Learn from the problem: once is a mistake . . . twice is stupid.
6. Erase it: Don't dwell on the problem. Forgive yourself and move on.

7. Replace it: Exchange positive experiences and information for negative experiences and information.
8. PUSH: Push until something happens!
9. Take responsibility: If it can be done, then it must be done.
10. Change your self-talk: Sweet talk yourself; speak "good" to yourself.

Part IV

The Power of Desire

◇ ◇ ◇ The last part of the VDAD formula is desire. It is absolutely necessary in turning your setbacks into comebacks. When we hear the word "desire" we usually think of things that we crave for, but there is much more to desire. Yes, desire does have a definition that includes cravings and satisfying appetites. Desire also includes those things that you earnestly long for, and the degree of intensity that you are willing to exert in reaching the goal you have set . . . or the degree of energy you are willing to expend in reaching your goal. In other words, how badly do you want to reach your goal and what are you willing to do in order to achieve your goal?

You must want to turn the setback into a setup for a comeback, and you must want it badly. How badly do you want to turn your setback into a setup for a comeback? Whenever I ask that question in my programs I always get the same answer, "Real bad!" Okay, but how bad is "real bad?" There are different levels of wanting something "real bad."

Have you ever woken up late at night and had a desire for a soda? We have all probably had that feeling at some point in our lives. Imagine a guy who wakes up around midnight and says, "I want a soda and I want it real bad!" This guy goes to the refrigerator and looks, but there are no sodas. He goes to the window, opens the shades and sees that it's snowing. He goes back to the refrigerator and looks again, but to no avail, so he settles for a glass of water and goes back to bed . . . he really didn't want it that bad!

Another guy wakes up around midnight and says, "I want a soda, and I want it real bad". This guy goes to the refrigerator and looks, but there are no sodas. He goes to the window, open up the shades and sees that it's snowing. This guy puts on his hat, coat, gloves and boots and walks a quarter mile to the corner store, but it's closed! So he walks back home and settles for a glass of orange juice, because he really didn't want it that bad!

Another guy wakes up around midnight and says "I want a soda, and I want it real bad." This guy goes to the refrigerator and looks, but there are no sodas. He goes to the window, opens the shade and sees that it's snowing. He puts on his hat and coat and gloves and boots and walks a quarter mile to the corner store, but it's closed! Then he walks another mile to the grocery store, but it too is closed! Then he walks another mile to the gas station with the soda machine, but it's sold out . . . but he keeps walking and trying, and walking and trying, and walking and trying until he gets a soda! Imagine, if you would go that far for a soda, how much further would you go for your dreams? That is a question only you can answer! How badly do you want it?

Desire is broken into three parts:

1. the desires of your heart, that are determined by your faith;
2. the desires of your mind, your level of focus and your commitment to achieve your goals;
3. the desires of your soul, which is your insight and attitude toward the setback and how you are serious about turning the setback into a setup for a comeback.

Let's start with the desires of your heart, which are determined by your faith, because faith is absolutely necessary in your quest to turn a setback into a comeback!

Step 8
....

Have Faith! You Are Blessed and Highly Favored!

If you can just believe. All things are possible to them that believe!

—Mark 9:23

He who loses money, loses much
He who loses a friend, loses more
He who loses faith, loses all

We go through life with a series of God ordained opportunities, brilliantly disguised as challenges.

—Charles Udall

◇ ◇ ◇ I believe that all the chapters of this book are important, but I truly believe that this is the most important chapter, because faith is critical to turning a setback into a setup for a comeback. Faith is critical because faith gives hope, and hope gives us an optimistic expectation for the future, and with an optimistic expectation of the future we are more apt to keep going in difficult times. If we are able to keep going in difficult times, then we will be able to effectively turn our setbacks into comebacks over and over again.

Faith gives us hope, and faith also gives us strength. It is a power source that allows us to keep going, specifically in tough times. And since we have come to the realization that we will all have some tough times, we need faith. You need faith, but where is your faith?

See, everyone has faith, unfortunately some have misplaced their faith. I know everyone has faith because I have looked at people as they go through their daily routines. I've seen how they apply their faith. Like the person who walks into a restaurant, pulls out a chair and then sits down, without checking to see if the chair can hold their weight. They have faith that the chair is able to do what it was created to do. Or the people who get on an airplane and take a seat without asking to see the pilot and checking his or her license. We have faith that the airline would only have a qualified, experienced person in the position of pilot. Another example is when people get a job and work for two weeks or even a month without any money from their employer because they have faith that the person will pay them at the appropriate time and that their check will be good. Faith! Everyone has faith!

Yes, everyone must have faith in order to exist in the world as we know it. But where is your faith? That's a powerful question that must be answered whenever you have a setback and want to turn it into a comeback. Where is it? Is it in the problem or is it in the solution to the problem. Is it in the present circumstances or is it in the future possibilities. Is it in your fears or is it in your faith. Is it in Murphy's Law or is it in God's promises? Where is your faith? I say have faith in a God who will help you to understand that those things that others mean for bad, He means for your good. Have faith in a God who can truly help you to see that a setback really is nothing but a setup for a comeback.

Joseph and the Coat of Many Colors

The biblical story of Joseph is probably one of the best stories ever about the power of a setback turning into a comeback. Joseph was a young man who was a dreamer. He was his father's favorite son, so he was given a coat of many colors. Joseph would share his dreams with his brothers, and they hated him because his dreams always showed him rising above them. One day they decided to get rid of this "dreamer" once and for all. When Joseph came out to the field his brothers threw him into a deep pit. They had planned to kill Joseph, so they took off his coat of many colors, threw animal blood on it, so they could take it back to their father and say that Joseph had been killed by a wild animal. While the brothers were trying to decide how best to kill him, a band of traders came along, so they sold Joseph to the traders. Joseph had a setback.

The traders took Joseph to Egypt and sold him to Potiphar, who was an officer of the Pharaoh, the king of Egypt. Joseph flourished as Potiphar's assistant, and everything he touched became a success. Soon he was put in charge of all of Potiphar's administrative affairs, and became Potiphar's favorite servant, but there was trouble brewing.

Potiphar's wife had romantic eyes for Joseph and consistently tried to seduce him and get him to sleep with her. Joseph consistently refused, but one day, when everyone else was out of the house, she caught Joseph by his robe and insisted he sleep with her. He ran but she was embarrassed and started screaming and accused Joseph of attempting to rape her. Potiphar believed her story and threw Joseph in jail. This was another setback for Joseph, but God knew a comeback was on the way!

While in jail Joseph became friendly with the chief jailer, who made him his main administrator. The chief jailer gave him responsibility over all of the other prisoners. Joseph became friends with two other inmates from the palace, the chief baker and the chief butler. One night they both had dreams that they could not understand so they asked Joseph to interpret the dreams. He told the butler that he would regain his stature in the Pharaoh's household. Then the chief baker got excited and asked what his dream meant. Joseph told him that his dream meant that he would be killed. It turned out that Joseph's predictions came true. The chief butler promised Joseph he would remember him when he was back in the Pharaoh's house and would get him out of jail, but he didn't. Another setback for Joseph.

Yet Joseph never lost his faith. He believed something good would come from all the misfortune. He continued to see a setback as nothing but a setup for a comeback. A few years later Pharaoh had a dream that none of his staff could interpret, then the chief butler remembered Joseph. Pharaoh sent for Joseph and told him about the dreams. Joseph not only was able to interpret the dreams but also gave him an action plan to overcome the challenges that were to come. The king was so taken by Joseph, and his faith, that he made him his personal assistant. Within a short time he was promoted to the director of all administrative activities in Egypt and then became the Pharaoh's second in command. At the age of thirty Joseph became the second most powerful person in Egypt and had control over all the allocations of property and supplies.

Joseph had predicted seven prosperous years that were to be followed by seven lean years, so he instructed the Egyptians to store food and supplies during the seven prosperous years in anticipation for the seven lean years. During the seven prosperous years Joseph's stature continued to grow, as did his faith. Following the seven prosperous years there was a famine, but the Egyptians had plenty because of Joseph's plan. The people in other neighboring countries were hit hard and many were on the brink of starvation. Joseph's brothers heard there was food in Egypt and decided to go to Egypt and try to buy some food there.

During this time Joseph was the governor of all Egypt. He was in charge of the sale of grain, therefore the brothers had to come and bow before Joseph and ask him for grain. Joseph recognized them but they did not recognize him.

He interrogated them and found out that their father was alive and well. He also found that he had a new, younger brother. He finally told them who he was and told them to go get their father and move their families to Egypt so they could have food and provisions during the famine.

Joseph forgave them for selling him into slavery because he said it was that act that eventually saved their lives. He told them that what others meant for bad, God meant for good. He showed them that a setback is nothing but a setup for a comeback, but you've got to have faith.

I say that to really become empowered to turn your problems you must have faith. Faith in a God who will never leave you nor forsake you. This story is one of my favorites about the fact that you are never alone if you just have faith.

The Country Doctor

Once there was an old country doctor who lived in a rural area. He would go from farmhouse to farmhouse taking care of the people and their illnesses. One day in the middle of summer his car broke down and he had to walk from farmhouse to farmhouse. At the end of that day he was so tired he could hardly put one foot before the other. He wearily came into his house and was so tired he didn't even want dinner, he just wanted to go to sleep. He went into his bedroom and laid down, and was asleep before his head hit the pillow. His wife came in and loosened his tie and unlaced his shoes and put his feet up on the bed.

About an hour later the phone rang and the doctor's wife answered it so it would not disturb the doctor. It was Mrs. Smith from the farmhouse down the road and she was hysterical because her baby had a high temperature and she didn't know what to do, she needed the doctor right away. The doctor's wife told her that the doctor was too tired to come right now, but to give the baby a cold compress and aspirin and the doctor would be there first thing in the morning. Even though he was in deep sleep, his subconscious recognized that there was someone who needed him. He wearily asked, "What's wrong?" His wife told him about the baby with the high temperature, and he got up and said he had to go see about the child.

He got his satchel and started to walk to Mrs. Smith's farm, which was about two miles away. As he walked to Mrs. Smith's farm he had to go through a tunnel. As he entered the dark tunnel a voice shouted out to him, "Hey, you got a match?" The doctor stopped and put down his satchel, pulled out a match, held it up close to his face so he could see it, struck the match, lit the man's cigarette, pulled the match back and blew it out.

He then went on to Mrs. Smith's house. He worked on the baby and was able to get the temperature down and gave her medicine to make her feel better. He then started back on his trek home. When he got back to that tunnel on his return trip he again encountered a man in the midst of the darkness. The man again shouted, "Hey, you got a match?" Again the doctor stopped and put down his satchel, pulled out a match, held it up close to his face so he could see it, struck the match, lit the man's cigarette, pulled the match back and blew it out. He hurried home and again fell into a deep sleep.

A few hours later the phone rang again. The doctor jumped up and caught the phone and gasped as he heard the information on the other end. It was the sheriff who said that Mr. Brown, one of the doctor's best friends was walking through the tunnel that night and someone jumped him, beat him, robbed him and left him for dead. He needed the doctor immediately if Mr. Brown was to be saved. The doctor quickly got his satchel and ran to the infirmary. He worked feverishly on

Mr. Brown and was able to stabilize him so they could get him to the hospital.

The doctor asked the sheriff, "Did you find who did this?" The sheriff said, "Yes, we have him over at the jail!" The doctor said, "Can I see him?" and the sheriff said, "Yes," and took him over to the jailhouse. When they got there the doctor was astonished, because behind the bars was the man he had encountered twice that night. The doctor went up to the cell and asked the man, "Why? Why didn't you hurt me?" The man replied, "It was my plan to not only rob you and beat you, but to kill you and steal all of your expensive medicines . . . but every time you lit the match, there was somebody standing next to you!"

Friends, you will have all kinds of encounters as you go along the way to do that which you have been commissioned to do. Some of these encounters will be frightening, and painful and difficult, but you must always stay faithful and remember that we have a promise that God will never leave you nor forsake you. He will always be beside you; just have faith.

What is faith? Scripture tells us that "Faith is the assurance of things hoped for, the evidence of things not seen." Scripture also tells us, "For God has not given us the spirit of fear, but of power, and of love, and of a sound mind." Unfortunately most people live their lives in a spirit of fear and not a spirit of faith. They allow fear to rest, rule and abide in their lives. They live their lives with fear at the helm, and faith as a stowaway. Live your life with faith at the wheel and I suggest that you cast fear overboard.

Psychiatrists have proven that there are only two fears that we were born with, the fear of falling and the fear of loud noises, every other fear is a learned behavior. Babies come to this earth with only those two fears and then are taught the other fears. My friend, Dale Smith Thomas shares in her speeches the meaning of FAITH versus FEAR! F-E-A-R stands for FALSE EVIDENCE APPEARING REAL, while F-A-I-T-H stands for FINDING ANSWERS IN THE HEART! What are the answers you will search and find in your heart?

The Famous Wally Amos!

Wally Amos has become a friend over the last few years. We have spoken on a number of programs together and found that we have a lot in common. Wally is a great example of someone who turned a setback into a setup for a comeback. His story is legendary and has come to be a standard of never giving up.

Wally Amos was born in Florida and grew up in New York. As a young man he became interested in the music industry and became a music agent. He quickly became a very successful agent. As a way of thanking his clients he would bake chocolate chip cookies and give them away. They became so popular that he started getting requests from lots of people. Many offered to buy the cookies, so he started selling them in little plastic bags. The requests came faster and faster and he soon had to make a decision, to either stay at his job, which he liked, or make cookies, which he loved. He decided to do what he loved and started a company called the Famous Amos Chocolate Chip Cookie Company.

He worked hard and in a few years people all over the country were buying Famous Amos chocolate chip cookies in stores across the country. He was a star! He started doing speeches and traveling and left the cookie business to run itself. Unfortunately businesses don't run themselves. Like cars they must have a driver or they will run off the road. The business got into financial difficulties so Wally started to look for a way to let someone else drive the runaway car. A company offered to buy the Famous Amos company and keep Wally as the spokesman. They said they would give him a great salary to keep his name in the headlines. Wally sold the company, lock, stock, barrel and name, Famous Amos Chocolate Chip Cookies.

Things were great for the first couple years then the company was sold to another company, which then sold it to another company, which then sold it to another, bigger company. By the time it got to the fourth owner they felt they didn't need Wally anymore and told him good-bye. But they decided they were going to keep the "Famous Amos" name, and told Wally that he couldn't use it anymore.

Wally told them that Famous Amos was his name and people around the world knew him by the name "Famous Amos". They couldn't take his name. They said "Oh yes we can. When you sold the company you signed a document giving the owner the rights to the name." Wally and the company ended up in court, and Wally lost. He had to give up the name Famous Amos and was told he would be sued if he even put his name on any promotional materials.

Wally went back to Hawaii to regroup. He was down, but he was not out. Wally knew that a setback is nothing but a setup for a comeback. Wally told his family that God is not a one-idea God. He said, "God gave me the first idea and I am confident that He will give me another." Wally soon got another idea and started a new company called "Uncle No-Name's Cookies and Muffins". The company is now starting to over-take the Famous Amos Cookies company. He also has become a best selling author and developed an infrastructure that allows him to speak and travel while people he trusts are driving the car.

Wally's steps to turn the setback into a setup for a comeback:

1. Remember God is not a one-idea God; if he gives you one idea He can and will give you another.

2. Remember God is greater than any situation you have. Have faith!

3. Always look for ways to turn lemons into lemonade.

4. Keep in mind there are no facts on the future. You create the facts!

5. It really doesn't matter where you came from, the key is where you are going.

6. Wally says "I reached for the sky, but missed . . . so I grabbed a few stars."

Have faith, which is stepping out on nothing and believing you will land on something. Focus is directing your energies on a project and creating a fire. Follow-through is taking consistent persistent action and making your dreams come true.

Wally proved that even a man with no name can turn a setback into a setup for a comeback.

Jane Fletcher White

Jane Fletcher White is an amazing lady from Houston, Texas, who has overcome a number of setbacks by utilizing her faith. Jane was a music major who graduated from college and got a job on a cruise line, singing in the theater group. After a year of singing on cruises, she settled in New York singing in theater groups. Eventually she got homesick and went back to Houston. While in Houston she met a man, who was the first man she met right off the plane, and a year later she was married to him.

The newlyweds worked hard to save money because they wanted to buy a home and start a family, but after a year of trying to start a family Jane was told that she could not have children. She was disappointed but continued to be grateful for all that she did have and continued to have faith that God could and would do something miraculous. A month later . . . she found out she was pregnant. Nine months later she delivered 15 pounds worth of babies, one boy and one girl! Then four months later she was pregnant again and a few months later she gave birth to a baby girl. She had three children in less than two years!

When the kids were still young Jane went for her checkup and was diagnosed with a very rare and very deadly form of cancer. The doctors gave Jane a few months to live. She again was at a critical juncture, but she remembered what God had done before and was confident he could and would do it again. In fact she was so confident that while in the hospital she made a point of going around and encouraging the other patients. Jane continued to have great faith and continued to believe God for a miracle.

Many of the doctors felt she was in a severe state of denial, but Jane was confident they were wrong . . . and they were! Twenty years later Jane is still here and is living life to the fullest. She is speaking to groups around the country, singing with a theater group and having a ball each and every day!

Jane said there were a number of major points she learned from her setbacks that were turned into comebacks.

1. Know it's okay to have shock initially and even some fear, but work quickly to displace the fear with faith. "Trust in the Lord, for He will see you through!"
2. Remain calm! Panic does not help in the process. It just makes things worse. Remain calm and have faith!
3. Put priorities in order. God, family, then everything else after that!
4. She learned to ask, "In the grand scheme of things is this important? If it is . . . then fight for it. If it is not . . . let it go!
5. Never take anybody, anything, or any day for granted!

6. Dare to take risks and try every open door. If one closes know that God will open another!

7. Have faith and trust in God.

There's No Place Like Home . . .
The Power of Faith, Focus and Follow-Through!

When you change your thinking you will change how you see things. I found that to be true one evening while watching television with my son. I read that *The Wizard of Oz* was being broadcast for the last time this century. Even though I had seen it dozens of times I decided to sit down with my son and watch it again. As we watched the great classic I saw the story from a different perspective, and saw things I had never seen before.

Once upon a time there was a little girl from Kansas named Dorothy. Dorothy got caught up in a storm and ended up far away from home, dazed, lost and confused. (I realized that this is a lot like life, sometimes we all will get caught up in storms and get off track and find ourselves in places and situations that are alien to us). She wanted to go home, but she didn't know how. (Have you ever gotten swept off track and ended up in a strange place where you felt lost and had no idea of where or how you should proceed?) She met a lot of new people and everyone wanted to give her advice on how to solve her problem. They said, "Go to see the Wizard . . . follow the Yellow Brick Road."

She set out on the quest and along the way she came upon a scarecrow. The scarecrow was a nice fellow, but he didn't have a brain, therefore he didn't have the ability to dream. He desperately wanted a brain, so Dorothy invited him to come along with her to see the Wizard, so they set off along the yellow brick road to let the Wizard make their dreams come true.

A little further down the road they encountered a tin man, who didn't have a heart, therefore he didn't have the capacity to believe in his dream. Dorothy told him about the Wizard and invited him to come along so the Wizard could give him a heart. Off they went along the Yellow Brick Road. Then they came upon a cowardly lion, who didn't have the courage to live his dream (because it definitely takes courage to live your dream). He wanted to be the king of the forest, but he was too afraid. They realized he needed courage to be the king of the forest, so they invited him to go along to see the Wizard.

Along they way they encountered obstacles and challenges and life-threatening situations, but they kept going because they felt that they needed the Wizard to make them complete. Finally after many tests and trials they got to see the Wizard, but found out that he was a fake, a phony, a pretender. He wasn't able to help them; in fact he was still trying to figure out how to get his own life together.

They were devastated. All their hard work was in vain. They had done so much to get to the Wizard, just to find that he was not able to help them get back home. As they cried over their problems, they got a visit from Glinda, the Good Witch. She looked at them with pity and said, "You didn't need the Wizard to go back home, you had it within you all the time. All you had to do was to click your heels together three times."

At that moment I thought of the wonderful quote from Emerson that states, "That which is before and that which is behind you can never compare with that which is within you!" In my mind's eye I could see the group standing there looking in amazement as Glinda utter those words, "It was within you all the time." In my mind I saw Glinda then giving them the formula for turning their challenges into opportunities. The formula for turning their problems into possibilities and turning their setbacks into setups for comebacks was with them all along. I closed my eyes and visualized her saying, "Just click your heels three times, once for vision, once for decision and once for action. And if you sincerely want it badly enough, you will go home." Dorothy clicked three times and she went home.

Friends, everything you need to make your dreams come true is already within you, just click your heels together three times. Click once for *faith*, which is the ability "to call forth those things that be not as though they are." "Faith is the willingness to jump . . . and grow wings on the way down." Occasionally we all get caught up in storms and might lose our way home. Take time to pray and seek guidance, and work on building your faith because it's like a muscle, the more you use it the stronger it gets. As you strengthen your faith you will be able to stand in the middle of the storms and not give up. Faith gives us the ability to believe that our dreams are possible.

In the Broadway adaptation of *The Wizard of Oz*, which was entitled, *The Wiz*, Glinda sang a song called "If You believe," right before showing them how to click their heels three times. She said if you believe within your heart, you can float on air and you can go home. You must believe if you want to turn your setbacks into comebacks. You must believe that you can and believe that you will. Develop the belief that it is impossible for you to fail, then act on that belief. Then you will not fail. You will have setbacks but you will no longer see them as failures but as setbacks, which are nothing but setups for comebacks.

Next you will click for *focus*. Focus on the possibilities, not on the problems. Focus on the positive perspective, not the negative perspective. Focus on your goals not on your obstacles. Focus your energies on the major issues at hand and not on all of the minor nuisances that will try to steal your time and energy. Focus on the options available to you. The person who is able to harness and focus their energies creates the fires of life, not by those whose energies are fractured and disjointed. Click for focus.

The third click is for *follow-through*, because you must take action if you want to turn your setbacks into comebacks. When you believe that you will find a way, and then act on those beliefs with the expectation that your actions will reap positive results, then you will start to fly. Unfortunately many people have faith but no follow-through. God gives the bird it's food, but He does not throw it into its nest. It takes faith and action, because faith without works is dead. Have faith, stay focused and follow-through: take action.

James Carter and Ramon Williamson have written a book called, *22 Uncommon Ways To Success*, in which one of the chapters says it wonderfully, "Walk by faith . . . but run when you can!" Friends, you need faith to turn a setback into a setup for a comeback, but it takes action. Faith and action, are a powerful team. Don't leave home without them! Just click your heels three times, with faith, focus and follow-through and remember . . . there's no place like home, there's no place like home, there's no place like home!

> *Faith is to believe what we do not see and the reward of faith is to see what we believe*
>
> —St. Augustine

Step 8—Teaching Points

1. Determine, where is your faith? Is it in God or in the circumstances?
2. What others meant for bad, God means for good. Just have faith.
3. Live your faith, not your fears.

4. FEAR versus FAITH = false evidence appearing real versus finding answers in the heart
5. God is not a one-idea God.
6. Stay "Blessed and Highly Favored." Speak it and live it!
7. Take count of your blessings, not your problems.
8. Be willing to bet on yourself even when others won't.
9. Faith is stepping out on nothing, and believing you will land on something.
10. Click your heels three times, once for faith, then for focus, then for follow-through and find the power deep inside of you and you will find your way home.

Step 9

It's All Good! Be Thankful!
Have an Attitude of Gratitude!

*All things work together for the good for those who love
the Lord and are called according to His purposes!*
—Romans 8:28

◇ ◇ ◇ Charles Spurgeon, the noted English clergyman, noticed that the weather vane on the roof of a farm building bore the phrase, "God is Love" and was troubled. "Do you think God's love is as changeable as that weather vane?" he asked the farmer. "You miss the point, good sir," replied the farmer. "It's on the weather vane because no matter which way the wind is blowing, God is still love." No matter which way the wind blows, its all good, because in time all things really do work together for the good.

In order to completely turn a setback into a setup for a comeback you must come to the conclusion that it is all good, It really is all good! Over the last few years the young people across America have established a new discourse which goes like this:

"How you doing?"

"Fine!"

"What's happening?"

"It's all good!"

"Yeah, it's all good!"

I do not know if they truly understand the power of that statement but I am glad that they are saying it, and therefore speaking it into being. No matter what happens in life, it's all good! It's a wonderful way to reply to life; just know it's all good! I shared a story in my first book that has gotten such a positive response that I must reprint it in this book. I think this so wonderfully illustrates that everything is "All Good" because truly all things really do work together for the good!"

All Things Work Together for Good . . .

Once upon a time there was a wise Chinese father in a small community. This wise father was held in high esteem, not so much because of his wisdom, but because of his two possessions: a strong son and a horse. One day the horse broke through the fence and ran away. All the neighbors came around and said, "What bad luck!" and the wise father replied, "Why do you call it bad luck?" A few days later the horse came back, with ten other horses, and all the neighbors said, "What good luck!" and the wise father responded, "Why do you call it good luck?" A few days later his strong son went out to the corral to break one of the new horses, and he was thrown and broke his hip. All the neighbors came over and said, "What bad luck!" and the wise father responded, "Why do you call it bad luck?"

About a week later the evil warlord came through the town and gathered all of the strong, able-bodied young men and took them off to war, the only one he did not take was the boy with the broken hip. All the young men were killed in battle, and when the news reached the community, the neighbors rushed to the father and said, "What good luck!" and the father said "Luck? No! It is not luck! All things work together for the good, for those who love the Lord!"

There may be times when things really look tough and when things do not go as you planned, but if you look hard enough and have faith, you will see that with every blessing there is a burden and with every burden, there is a blessing. Every dark cloud has a silver lining, if you are willing to look for it and learn from it.

The Power Of Vision, Decision, Action, Desire and Faith!

Sometimes in life we have teeth-rattling experiences and we run to God because our world is shaking, only to find out that it is God who is doing the shaking.

—Author Unknown

Ain't no use in crying when it's raining, cause crying only adds to the rain! Ain't no use in worrying about your problems, cause worrying only adds to the pain! See life's got ups just like it's got downs. And life's got smiles just like it's got frowns.

—Rance Allen

Focus on the Solution, Not on the Problem!

When you have a setback you must focus your energies. Unfortunately most people focus on the problem and not on the solution. They take their eyes off the goal and focus on the challenges all around the goal. They spend all of their time worrying about the problem and very little time thinking about the solution. If you are going to think about and dwell on things that might happen, that are yet to happen, why not think about the good things that can happen, the positive things that can happen?

Worry does not solve problems; it usually adds to them. Worrying is a misuse of the imagination. Most people worry themselves into bad health, which creates more problems and more worries. Medical experts agree that most disease it not so much what you eat, but rather what is eating you. Worrying never solves the problem. Do not focus your energies on the problem, because the problem is already here. Focus on creating solutions and then acting on the solutions. The solution is waiting to be born, waiting to be discovered, waiting to be uncovered, but you must bring it to life. Act and unleash the wonderful answers that will make the problem a thing of the past and will make the solution a thing of the present.

In life we will have challenges, we will have problems, we will have setbacks. Just keep in mind that there is no use in crying when it's raining and there is no use in worrying about the problems. Focus your energy on the solution and not on the problem and remember that a setback is nothing but a setup for a comeback!

Even though we will all go through challenging times, do not despair, have faith, hold on and realize that we will understand it better by and by. I look back and realize that I did not understand it when I was fired from my singing job. I did not understand it when I was delegated to a desk job after having success speaking for the school system. They were all setbacks. I did not understand why then, but in time I understood it much better.

If I had not been fired from my singing job and replaced by a karaoke machine, I would not have taken a job with the school system. If I had not taken a job with the school system I probably would not have started speaking. If I had never started speaking I would have never joined the National Speakers Association. If I had not joined the National Speakers Association, I would not have been invited to speak at the 1994 National Speakers Association Convention. If I had not been invited to speak at that Convention I would not have met book publicist, Rick Frishman. If Rick Frishman had not heard me speak, then he would not have referred me to literary agent, Jeff Herman. If I had never been referred to Jeff Herman he would never have been able to negotiate a book deal with St. Martin's Press. And if there were no book deal, *you* would not be reading this book!

And it all started with a setback, a setback of being fired from a singing job and being replaced by a karaoke machine. That led to another setback on my job with the school system, where I had to make a decision whether to do what was necessary or do what was comfortable. I decided to quit and walk by faith. From there I started speaking and created a one-minute radio show that created a book of one-minute motivation. And now there is a book about turning setbacks into comebacks. And this all started with a setback. Oh, yes I do finally understand that a setback is nothing but a setup for a comeback!

I didn't understand it then, but I understand it now. If I just have faith and keep going and keep the vision clearly in sight, and am willing to fight for my dreams then my setbacks will become stepping-stones to my dreams. I have found it to be true; a setback really is nothing but a setup for a comeback. No matter what happens . . . it's all good!

The Burning Hut!

The only survivor of a shipwreck was washed up on a small, uninhabited island. He prayed feverishly for God to rescue him, and every day he scanned the horizon for help, but none seemed forthcoming. Exhausted, he eventually managed to build a little hut out of driftwood to protect him from the elements, and to store his few possessions.

But then one day while scavenging for food, he saw a flash of lightning. He arrived home to find his little hut in flames, with the dark smoke rolling up to the sky. The worst had happened; everything was lost. He was stung with grief and anger. "God, how could you do this to me!" he cried. Yet, somewhere in his pain he found the strength to say, "I must continue to have faith, I must continue to have faith." Early the next day he was awakened by the sound of a ship that was approaching the island. It had come to rescue him. "How did you know I was here?" asked the weary man of his rescuers. "It was your smoke signal," they replied.

Friends, It is easy to get discouraged when things are going bad. But we shouldn't lose heart, because God is at work in our lives, even in the midst of the challenges. Remember next time your little hut is burning to the ground——it just may be a smoke signal that turns your life around. Your world is shaking and you run to God . . . only to find out that it is God is doing the shaking. Well, God's in the shaking; God's in the breaking, but always remember, God's in the making!

Have faith, believe in your dreams and take action and always remember that setbacks are a part of life, and setbacks are going to happen, whether you like them or not. So get a new perspective. Realize it only takes a minute to change your life and turn it around. The minute you make a decision, take action, move toward your vision and do so with great desire, you will change your life and start turning your setbacks into comebacks. Remember it takes Vision, Decision, Action and Desire. If you can do this, you too will be able to say "Oh what a wonderful minute . . . A setback is nothing but a setup for a comeback, and I'm coming back!" Do it now! It is within your grasp. God Bless!

Step 9—Teaching Points

1. No matter what happens, it's all good!
2. All things work together for the good.
3. Ain't no use in crying when it's raining; focus on the solution not the problem.
4. Have an attitude of gratitude.
5. Sometimes it's God who is doing the shaking as well as the making.
6. Worry never solves any problem, but action does.
7. Choose to win! Choose to be healthy, wealthy, wise, happy and thankful.
8. Your burning hut may be a smoke signal for greater success.
9. Vision, Decision, Action and Desire are a powerful team. Don't leave home without them.
10. It only takes a minute to make a comeback. The minute you decide and take action you're on your way!

Epilogue

◇ ◇ ◇ This book has been a labor of love. It has been challenging and difficult and I have had a number of setbacks in the process. I have had to write, rewrite, then rewrite again. I have had major computer problems and time crunches and setbacks. I have had heartaches because I was unable to get on paper what I had in my heart, yet I continued on and I refused to give up. And I have grown because of it. I am confident that the person I am now, at the end, is a much different person from the person I was at the beginning of this process.

I pray that I have reached my objectives. My first objective was to inspire you. I hope that this book has been able to "breathe anew" and inspire you with new ideas and new insights into how to view setbacks and problems in your life. I hope that you have been inspired as well as motivated; therefore you will not only be moved in a motivational sense, with your mind, but also be inspired and compelled to act because of issues from your heart.

My second objective was to give you some information. Motivation and inspiration without information is incomplete. I hope that this has been a complete manual. I hope you have been given some good "How to's", some "A-Ha's" and "Teaching Points" that will illuminate effective TIPS (techniques, ideas, principles and strategies) for success.

My third objective was to share my philosophy and some of my theological perspectives in a way that was simple yet enlightening. I wanted to make it simple enough that a child could read it and understand it, yet informative and complex enough that a college scholar could read it and enjoy it. It was difficult but I have tried to make it a book that would be of help to a great number of people, who could understand and absorb the information and go on and effectively turn their setbacks into comebacks.

Finally I desperately wanted to share my faith with others and get them to read my heart, not just my words. I am so thankful for what God has done in my life, and I don't know if you are a Christian, a Muslim, Jewish or of any other faith or religious persuasion, but just as I would share with friends a great restaurant or a great movie I too wanted to share the joy and fulfillment I have received as a result of making a commitment to my faith. If you have finished this book and still have no one to call on, no one to pray to, no one who you can feel comfortable calling your God, then let me make a recommendation. This is someone who has helped me and has shown me that a setback is nothing but a setup for a comeback.

> *There was a young man who died in his early thirties after a brief public career had brought him fame in his time and territory. The tragic element of his life story is that after stunning success he was falsely accused of a crime that resulted in his imprisonment, trial and execution. The death penalty was carried out. The end of his life was utter disgrace, humiliation, and shame. I weep as I think of the whole sad, sordid spectacle of this social injustice, except that his name was eventually vindicated. He came back and his comeback was stunning and spectacular. His honor was restored and elevated. His name today is the most respected and renowned name in the Christian world.*

*Today we even count the years by him, time before
his death and time after his death. He is the King of
Comebacks . . . His name is Jesus and he is my friend
and inspiration. I know if you will just call . . . He will
answer! Just try Him, I am sure you will like Him.*

—Adapted from Dr. Robert Schuller

Thanks for reading and sharing with me the thoughts of my heart. I pray that you will share this information with others, who will share it with others and the process will continue and people can see, in massive numbers, that a "bend in the road is not the end of the road!" Go forth and live your dreams, with power, passion and purpose. And remember you were born for a reason and with a mission and you must live it!

Always stay blessed and highly favored, even in the midst of the challenges. I leave you with this quote by Nelson Mandela, "The greatest power in life is not ever falling, but in rising every time you fall." Keep rising! Go forth and remember that "A setback truly is nothing but a setup for a comeback!"

Remember:

*You have Only Just A Minute,
Only sixty seconds in it
Forced upon You, can't refuse it,
Didn't seek it, Didn't choose it
But it's up to You to use it,
You must suffer if you lose it
Give account if You abuse it,
Just a tiny little minute, but an Eternity is in it!*

You will have setbacks, but don't despair because a Setback really is Nothing but a Setup for a Comeback! Go Forward and Live Your Dreams!